THE WI BOOK OF
WHOLEFOOD
COOKERY

MARGARET HANFORD

EBURY
PRESS

ACKNOWLEDGEMENTS

Illustrated by Vanessa Luff
Edited by Sue Parish
Designed by Kim Church Associates and Clare Clements
Cover photography by James Jackson
The publishers would like to thank Professor Malcolm
Woodbine, formerly of the Dept. of Food Science and
Applied Biochemistry at the University of Nottingham's
School of Agriculture, for his advice.

Published by Ebury Press Ltd.,
National Magazine House,
72 Broadwick Street,
London W1V 2BP

ISBN 0 85223 472 4

First impression 1985

Filmset by
D.P. Media Ltd., Hitchin, Hertfordshire

Reproduced, printed and bound in Great Britain by
Hazell, Watson & Viney Ltd.,
Member of the BPCC Group, Aylesbury, Bucks.

CONTENTS

Introduction   4

Appetisers, soups and starters   12
Pâtés, vegetable soups, party nibbles,
savoury and fruit cocktails.

Main course dishes   24
Meat, fish, rice, pasta, lentil, nut,
vegetable, cheese and egg dishes.

Vegetables and salads   54
Hot and cold vegetable combinations;
potato dishes; mixed salads with nuts,
rice, beans and fresh vegetables.

Puddings and sweets   64
Fruit dishes, trifle, cheesecake,
custards and flans.

Baking with whole grains   74
Breakfast cereals, tea loaves, breads,
scones, croissants, cakes and biscuits.

Dressings and sauces   90
Salad dressings and sauces to
accompany main course or vegetable
dishes.

What is the WI?   94
About the author

Index   95

INTRODUCTION

Wholefoods are natural foods to which nothing has been added or taken away. They contain no artificial colourings, flavourings, preservatives or other additives and they are used in wholefood cookery in such a way as to retain their nutrients and natural flavours.

It is not necessary to become a vegetarian to enjoy a wholefood diet or to put into practice the methods of cooking recommended in this book. However, many people are now including more vegetarian dishes in their diet for health reasons, and so this book includes many recipes suitable for vegetarians, and also shows how other recipes can be adapted for vegetarians.

Vegetarians who include dairy products in their diet are known as lacto-vegetarians, but those who cut out all animal products, including milk, milk products and eggs etc. from their food, are known as vegans. Those recipes in this book suitable for vegans are clearly marked, as are the vegetarian recipes.

Key

Recipes marked	are suitable for:
V	Lacto-vegetarians
VV	Vegans and lacto-vegetarians

Recipes marked	can be adapted for:
(V)	Lacto-vegetarians
(VV)	Vegans and lacto-vegetarians

Fresh foods
Fresh fruits and vegetables from your own garden or from a self-pick farm, which can be picked and eaten when they are at their best, are first class value. It is still possible to buy really fresh fruit and vegetables from self-service supermarkets, or from market stalls and smaller shops rather than those sold in bags under hot lights in some of the supermarkets. Try to shop where there is a quick turn-over of food; in this way you should get fresher produce.

It is also possible to ensure that you get only fresh meat and fish by getting to know your suppliers and asking their advice. If you have to shop in supermarkets, seek out the latest 'sell-by' dates and avoid 'special offers' on meat and fish – they may be old, and beginning to deteriorate.

A balanced diet

'You are what you eat,' says Professor Yudkin, and in order to be fit and well and enjoy a sense of vitality, it is essential to eat a balanced diet as well as taking plenty of exercise and getting an adequate amount of sleep.

The food we eat can be divided into five groups:

Group 1: meat, fish, cheese and eggs; pulses, seeds and nuts (if combined with eggs, milk or cheese)

Group 2: fresh fruit

Group 3: vegetables, including pulses (e.g. peas, beans, lentils)

Group 4: whole grains, rice, bread, cereals or pasta

Group 5: milk and milk products (e.g. cheese, yoghurt and butter)

A well-balanced diet includes at least two helpings from *each* of these groups every day. (The amount of each helping needed by a person depends on their age and level of activity. For anyone trying to lose weight it is a good idea to eat a little less of each food rather than to cut out particular foods completely, otherwise their diet may become unbalanced.)

Eat raw fruit and vegetables whenever possible and try to include potatoes and a green vegetable in at least one meal a day. (Potatoes cooked in their skins taste better and contain more nutrients than those that have been peeled.)

Adults need at least 275 ml (½ pint) milk, and children at least 575 ml (1 pint) milk or milk products every day, but the lower fat content milks are now increasingly recommended, and for cooking purposes, skimmed milk rather than full fat milk can be used.

A good diet also includes plenty of fresh water – at least 6 glasses a day, either in the form of pure water, or, for example, as tea, are recommended.

Fibre

Eating habits have changed over the years, and since the last war, the development of modern food processing methods has meant that we eat more refined foods like white sugar, white bread and other refined cereals. These foods have been treated in such a way that the fibre in them has been lost.

Fibre helps our digestive systems to function normally. It is not broken down during digestion, but it helps to remove other waste products from the body regularly, preventing constipation and other problems. Constipation can often be cured by increasing the fibre in our diets. This means eating plenty of fruit, vegetables, nuts, pulses and bran.

Wholemeal flour and brown rice are rich in fibre and can be used to replace their refined equivalents. Homemade wholemeal or granary bread has a superb texture and flavour and is very satisfying to make.

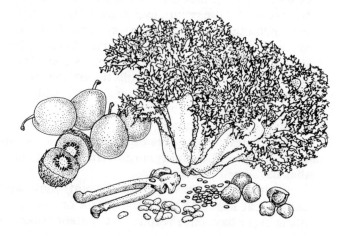

Flour
There are many types of flour that are suitable for home baking. This can be confusing for inexperienced cooks, so here is a classification of wheat flours which explains the differences behind the labels:

100% wholemeal or whole wheatmeal flour. This is often labelled 'stoneground' and is made from the whole grain of the wheat. Nothing has been added or extracted.

Wheatmeal flour. This may also be stoneground, but some of the bran and wheatgerm has been removed to give 81–90% whole grain content. 'Farmhouse' bread flour has 81% extraction and 'Country Cookbook' wheatmeal flour has 85% extraction.

Strong plain white bread flour. This has 70–73% extraction. During the milling process, all but a tiny trace of bran and wheatgerm are automatically sifted out from the ground grain.

Wheatgerm flour. Some proprietary brands of flour are milled, the bran and wheatgerm are removed, and then the wheatgerm is replaced at the end of the milling process. This is wheatgerm flour, and contains 80% of the original wheat grain.

Granary flour is the proprietary name of a blend of wheatmeal, rye flour and wheatflakes.

Fats
In Western countries, where animal products form a large part of the diet, people eat too much rich, fatty food, which may be high in cholesterol. It is important not only to cut down on fat, but to vary the diet, using pulses which are rich in protein to supplement the protein provided by meat.

It is also advisable, where possible, to choose corn, sunflower seed or vegetable oils and margarines instead of those made from animal fats, for frying and baking. Essential unsaturated fatty acids found in these vegetable oils and fats do not raise the blood cholesterol level. Saturated fatty acids found in animal fats, lard, dripping, butter, cream and cheese, tend to raise the level of cholesterol in the blood and this can eventually lead to a blockage of the coronary arteries, and thus be a contributory factor in coronory heart disease.

Carbohydrates

Our energy comes from the carbohydrates we eat, and we can obtain all the energy we require from natural foods such as vegetables, grains and pulses. If sweetening is required, it is worth remembering that white sugar provides nothing but 'empty' calories, and has no other nutritional value. Honey, molasses and muscovado sugar are a wiser choice because they contain very small quantities of mineral elements.

Fruits contain natural sugar (fructose) and dried fruits such as apricots, currants, raisins, sultanas, prunes and figs provide fibre and valuable nutrients as well.

Proteins

Proteins are required for the growth and repair of the body. The protein-rich foods include milk, fish, meat, eggs, nuts, cheese, grains and pulses.

Protein for vegans is obtained mainly from nuts, grains and pulses, and flavours can be enhanced by using yeast extract and Shoyu soya sauce (a fermented soya sauce) as well as fresh or dried herbs.

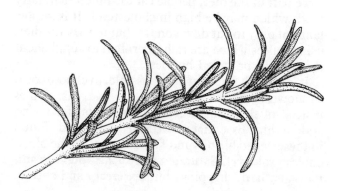

Vitamins and minerals

Vitamins are a large group of naturally occurring chemicals which perform a wide variety of functions in the body.

Vitamin A is needed for good vision, healthy skin and the linings of the bronchial tubes and throat. Liver, margarine and fish liver oils are excellent sources; carrots and dark green leafy vegetables are also a valuable source.

Vitamin B. There are a group of vitamins known as the B group, and these include thiamin, riboflavin, B_6 and B_{12}. They are important in the part they play in the release of energy from carbohydrates, fats and proteins, and they are involved with the working of the nervous system. Different B vitamins are found in cereals, yeast products, liver, kidney, wholewheat flour, nuts, fish, milk, green vegetables, and eggs. Vegans can encounter problems if they have insufficient vitamin B_{12} in their diets, because this is found essentially in animal products; however, it is possible to buy vitamin tablets to correct this deficiency reasonably cheaply.

Vitamin C is essential for body tissues; it helps to cement cells together and also helps in the process of healing wounds. It is found in citrus fruits, blackcurrants, rose hips, watercress, cabbage, tomatoes and potatoes. It is destroyed by light, oxygen and heat. Linus Pauling's work on the beneficial effects of large doses of vitamin C are well known. He has argued that large daily doses 'will promote longer life, cure infections such as the common cold and improve mental alertness'.

Vitamin D is sometimes called the sunshine vitamin because, provided we get sunshine, we produce compounds in our skin that are changed into vitamin D. Without sunshine, we can obtain vitamin D from fatty fish like herrings, sardines and tuna, and from dairy products.

Vitamin E is present in oils derived from cereals, e.g. wheat germ oil and corn oil; eggs are a rich source.

Relatively little is known of its importance to man. *Vitamin K* is found in green leafy vegetables, yoghurt and fish liver oil. It is known to play a part in the mechanism of blood clotting.

These are just a few examples of the sources and importance of vitamins, and a mixed, well-balanced diet provides the whole range of our needs. We also need a variety of *minerals* such as iron, which is a component of red blood cells, which carry oxygen to all the cells of the body. It is found in red meat, liver, dried apricots and wholemeal flour. Calcium is required for strong bones and teeth, and is found in milk and milk products.

In general, vitamins cannot function in our bodies without essential minerals, and some vitamins are needed to help the absorption of some minerals.

Methods of cooking
In order to retain the maximum nutrients and flavour in vegetables and fruit, steam rather than boil them. In the same way, grilling meat and fish is preferable to frying.

Many foods are delicious eaten raw; never be afraid to experiment with salads including raw vegetables. Some cooking inevitably destroys some of the value of these foods; for example, vitamin B_1 (thiamin) is destroyed by heat – vitamin C is also; its loss begins as soon as fresh fruit or vegetables are cut and left open to light and air.

One habit which nutritionists suggest we try and break is adding salt to foods; wherever possible, it is advisable to use herbs to flavour food instead. Too much salt (sodium chloride) in our diet, among other harmful effects, makes potassium unavailable to the body, and this can lead to fatigue.

Salt has not been taken out of the recipes in this book, because the amount used can vary according to personal tastes. Where preferred, it can be left out of most recipes or only a small amount used.

Measurements

All recipes are given in metric and imperial quantities. When following the recipes, use either metric measurements or imperial: do not mix the two.

Eggs are size 2 or 3 unless stated otherwise.

All spoon measurements are level unless stated otherwise.

American equivalents

	Metric	Imperial	American
Margarine	225 g	8 oz	1 cup
Cheese (grated)	100 g	4 oz	1 cup
Flour	100 g	4 oz	1 cup
Currants	150 g	5 oz	1 cup
Rice	225 g	8 oz	1 cup

An American pint is 16 fl oz compared with the imperial pint of 20 fl oz. A standard American cup measure is considered to hold 8 fl oz.

APPETISERS, SOUPS AND STARTERS

This chapter contains a selection of unusual
first course dishes, using fresh fruit and
vegetables as well as nuts, fish and cheese.

This chapter includes appetisers to serve before a meal, hot and cold soups and starters. Some accompaniments and serving suggestions appear at the ends of the recipes.

Soaking pulses

Dried pulses (peas, beans and lentils) must be soaked before they are cooked. Once cooked, they can be frozen for use later. They can be soaked in any of the following ways, depending on the time available.

Method 1. Put 225 g (8 oz) dried pulses into a saucepan with 575 ml (1 pint) cold water. Bring to the boil and cook for 2 minutes. Remove from the heat and leave the pulses to soak for 1 hour.

Method 2. Put 225 g (8 oz) dried pulses into a bowl. Pour in 575 ml (1 pint) boiling water. Soak the pulses for 2 hours.

Method 3. Put 225 g (8 oz) dried pulses into a bowl. Pour in 575 ml (1 pint) cold water and soak for 8–12 hours.

The third method gives the best results, but takes the longest.

PEANUT APPETISERS   VV

100 g (4 oz) peanuts or sunflower seeds
2 tbsp Shoyu soy sauce

Heat the oven to 100°C (200° F) mark ½. Coat the peanuts or sunflower seeds with the sauce. Place on a baking tray in the oven and stir frequently until dry and roasted.

SAVOURY WALNUT SABLÉS   V

Makes 24

75 g (3 oz) sunflower margarine
40 g (1½ oz) plain wholemeal flour
40 g (1½ oz) soft white flour
75 g (3 oz) finely grated cheese
salt and pepper
beaten egg to glaze
40 g (1½ oz) walnuts, coarsely
   chopped
rock salt

Heat the oven to 190°C (375° F) mark 5.
Grease and line two 20 x 30-cm (12 x 8-inch)
baking trays with greased greaseproof
paper. Rub the margarine into the flours;
add the cheese and seasoning and knead
together into a paste. Roll out to a thickness
of 2 mm (¹/₁₀ inch) and cut into strips about
5 cm (2 inches) wide. Brush with beaten egg
and sprinkle with walnuts. Grind a little
rock salt over the top. Cut each strip into
triangles, place on the prepared tins and
bake for 10–15 minutes.

These sablés are suitable for buffet snacks.

Variation
As an alternative, add 1 tablespoonful
chopped chives and 1 tablespoonful
chopped parsley to the mixture and replace
the chopped walnuts with sesame seeds.

SAVOURY COCKED HATS

Makes 16

50 g (2 oz) sunflower margarine
100 g (4 oz) plain wholemeal flour
   (or half wholemeal, half white)
50 g (2 oz) finely grated cheese
salt
pepper
good pinch of cayenne pepper
egg and water mixture (equal parts)

Filling
50 g (2 oz) smoked haddock
25 g (1 oz) grated cheese
½ tsp paprika

Heat the oven to 200°C (400° F) mark 6.
Grease a baking tray. Rub the fat into the
flour until it resembles fine breadcrumbs.
Add the cheese and seasoning. Add enough
egg and water mixture to form a fairly stiff
dough, reserving some for the filling. Roll
out and cut into 5-cm (2-inch) rounds.
   Cook the smoked haddock in water in a
frying pan to remove some of the salt. Strain
off the water. Flake the fish; mix with the
cheese, paprika and a little of the egg and
water mixture. Place the filling in the centre
of the rounds and dampen the edges with
water. Knock up the edges of the pastry and
fold inwards over the filling to form

triangles, leaving a little of the fish showing.

Brush with the egg and water mixture, place on the tray and bake for 10–15 minutes. Remove and place on a cooling rack and dust with paprika.

Any cooked or canned fish can replace the smoked haddock.

NUT PÂTÉ   (V)

Serves 6

75 g (3 oz) bacon
225 g (8 oz) onions
1 tbsp corn or sunflower oil
1 clove garlic, crushed
225 g (8 oz) mixed nuts (walnuts,
    hazelnuts, Brazil nuts and
    peanuts)
100 g (4 oz) wholewheat
    breadcrumbs
2 tbsp chopped fresh parsley or 2 tsp
    dried parsley
2 tbsp chopped fresh sage or 2 tsp
    dried sage
salt and pepper
1 egg, beaten

Heat the oven to 190°C (375° F) mark 5. Grease a 450-g (1-lb) loaf tin. Dice the bacon; peel and dice the onions. Heat the oil in a saucepan and fry the onions, bacon and garlic until the onion is lightly coloured. Remove from the pan and stir in the chopped mixed nuts. Add the breadcrumbs, herbs and seasoning and mix well. Add the egg to the mixture and mix thoroughly.

Turn into the tin and bake for 45 minutes or until brown. Turn out on to a warmed serving dish and serve with tomato sauce (see page 93). Alternatively, leave to cool in the tin and serve cold with salads.

Omit the bacon for a vegetarian dish.

HUMMUS V

Serves 4

100 g (4 oz) chick peas, soaked
1 clove garlic, crushed
rind and juice of ½ lemon
salt and pepper
150 ml (¼ pint) natural yoghurt

Garnish
4 lettuce leaves, shredded
2 tsp chopped chives
4 slices lemon
paprika

Soak the chick peas overnight in 275 ml (½ pint) water and place with the soaking water and garlic in a saucepan. Bring to the boil and simmer gently for about 2 hours until soft. Drain the chick peas, reserving the liquid. Cool and mash the chick peas, then stir in the rind and juice of lemon, salt, pepper and yoghurt. Beat or liquidise until smooth. If the mixture is too stiff, add some of the reserved cooking liquid.

Serve on individual plates on a bed of lettuce. Garnish with chopped chives, lemon slices and paprika.

RED BEAN SOUP VV

Serves 6

100 g (4 oz) red kidney beans
2 tbsp corn or sunflower oil
1 medium onion, diced
1 celery stalk, diced
1 medium carrot, diced
2 tomatoes, skinned and chopped
1 tbsp tomato purée
1 tsp chopped fresh oregano or ½ tsp
    dried oregano
1 tsp chopped fresh thyme, or ½ tsp
    dried thyme
1 bayleaf
900 ml (1½ pints) vegetable stock or
    water
freshly ground black pepper
6 tbsp chopped chives or parsley to
    garnish

Soak the beans overnight (or see page 13 for alternative methods). Drain well. Heat the oil in a large pan; add the onion, celery and carrot and cook until softened. Add the remaining ingredients. Bring to the boil and simmer for 1 hour. Adjust the seasoning and pour into a warmed soup tureen. Sprinkle with parsley or chives before serving.

CARROT SOUP (V)

Serves 4–6

50 g (2 oz) sunflower margarine
450 g (1 lb) carrots, diced
1 medium potato, diced
1 mediun onion, diced
850 ml (1½ pints) chicken stock
salt and freshly ground pepper
1 tsp curry powder (optional)
juice of ½ lemon
chopped parsley to garnish

Melt the fat and sauté the carrot, potato and onion for 5 minutes. Add the stock, curry powder, if used, and seasoning and cook for 20 minutes. Liquidise or sieve the soup. Return to the pan, add the lemon juice and adjust the seasoning. Bring to the boil, adding more water if necessary.

Pour into a warmed tureen and sprinkle with chopped parsley.

For a vegetarian soup, use water or vegetable stock instead of chicken stock.

MUSHROOM SOUP (V)

Serves 4–6

25 g (1 oz) sunflower margarine
25 g (1 oz) plain wholemeal flour
275 ml (½ pint) milk
575 ml (1 pint) chicken stock
225 g (8 oz) mushrooms
salt and freshly ground pepper
juice of ½ lemon
finely chopped parsley to garnish

Place the margarine, flour and milk in a saucepan. Whisk over a moderate heat until the sauce thickens. Add the chicken stock, finely chopped mushrooms, seasoning and lemon juice, and cook for 5 minutes. Pour into a warmed tureen and sprinkle with parsley before serving.

For a vegetarian soup, use water instead of chicken stock.

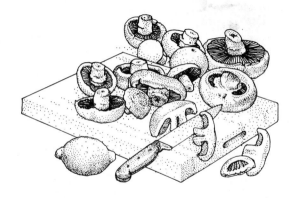

BRUSSELS SPROUT SOUP (V)

Serves 4

575 ml (1 pint) white stock e.g.
  chicken
450 g (1 lb) Brussels sprouts
salt and pepper
15 g (½ oz) cornflour
150 ml (¼ pint) milk
25 g (1 oz) sunflower margarine
finely chopped parsley to garnish

Bring the stock to the boil and add the prepared sprouts. Add the seasoning and cook until the sprouts are tender, then liquidise or sieve. Slake the cornflour with the milk and add to the soup. Bring to the boil. Cut the margarine into small pieces and add. Continue simmering for 2 minutes, stirring constantly. Pour into a warmed tureen, garnish with parsley and serve with Melba toast.

Use water or vegetable stock instead of white stock for a vegetarian soup.

BEAN SOUP (VV)

Serves 4

225 g (8 oz) dried butter beans
25 g (1 oz) sunflower margarine
1 onion, finely diced
4 celery stalks, diced
1 large carrot, cut into rings
850 ml (1½ pints) beef stock
juice and finely grated rind of
  ½ lemon
1 bay leaf
salt and pepper
1 tbsp chopped parsley to garnish

Soak the beans overnight in 575 ml (1 pint) water. Drain the beans and reserve the water. Melt the margarine in a large saucepan and sauté the onion, celery and carrot for 5 minutes. Add the soaking liquid to the stock to make it up to 1.2 litres (2 pints). Pour into the saucepan with the beans, lemon juice and rind and the bay leaf.

Cover the pan and bring to the boil. Either reduce the heat and simmer gently for 2 hours until the beans are tender or pour into a large vacuum flask and leave overnight until the beans are soft. Liquidise the soup. Return to the pan and reheat. Season, add the chopped parsley and more stock if necessary.

Use water or vegetable stock to make this a vegan recipe.

CUCUMBER AND YOGHURT SOUP   V

Serves 4–6

1 large cucumber
1 clove garlic, crushed (optional)
2 tbsp wine vinegar or distilled
    vinegar
1 tbsp fresh mint or chives, finely
    chopped
275 ml (½ pint) natural yoghurt
salt and freshly ground black pepper
275 ml (½ pint) milk, chilled
2 tbsp parsley, finely chopped, to
    garnish

Wash the cucumber and grate on a medium-sized grater. Transfer to a mixing bowl. Add the garlic, if used, together with the vinegar, mint or chives and yoghurt. Season and chill thoroughly. Just before serving, fold in the milk. Pour into chilled soup bowls and serve sprinkled with parsley.

CHILLED TOMATO SOUP   VV

Serves 4–6

450 g (1 lb) ripe tomatoes
1 medium onion, finely chopped
1 clove garlic, crushed
2 stems marjoram or oregano
2 basil leaves
salt and pepper
2 tbsp parsley, finely chopped

Skin the tomatoes and place in a saucepan with all the other ingredients except the parsley. Bring to the boil and simmer until the onions are tender, then liquidise or purée in a food processor. Place in a bowl and chill. Serve in individual bowls with small squares of toast, garnished with parsley.

PRAWN AND APPLE COCKTAIL

Serves 4

2 dessert apples
juice of 1 lemon
350 g (12 oz) peeled prawns
275 ml (½ pint) mayonnaise (see
    page 92
2 tbsp natural yoghurt
2–3 lettuce leaves
parsley to garnish

Peel, core and finely chop the apples and mix with the lemon juice. Add the prawns, reserving 4 for the garnish. Stir the apple and prawn mixture into the mayonnaise and yoghurt. Arrange on a bed of finely chopped lettuce leaves in individual cocktail glasses and garnish with the reserved prawns and parsley.

PEAR AND WALNUT SALAD   V

Serves 4

1 egg
1½ tbsp soft brown sugar
2 tbsp wine vinegar
2–3 drops tarragon vinegar
  (optional)
75 ml (3 fl oz) natural yoghurt
4 pears
8 lettuce leaves
50 g (2 oz) shelled walnuts

To prepare the dressing, beat the egg and sugar until thoroughly mixed, then add the vinegars. Place the bowl over a saucepan of gently simmering water and stir until the mixture is thick. Remove from the heat and leave until cold. Fold the yoghurt into the dressing.

Cut the pears in half and core. Place two halves per portion on lettuce leaves on a salad plate and immediately spoon the dressing over. Chop the walnuts roughly and scatter over the pears. Serve with buttered wholemeal bread.

For really thin slices of brown bread, remove the crusts from thin- or medium-sliced bread and roll each piece firmly with a rolling pin before spreading with butter or sunflower margarine.

PEARS WITH COTTAGE CHEESE   V

Serves 4

50 g (2 oz) Cheshire cheese, grated
150 ml (¼ pint) natural yoghurt
150 g (5 oz) cottage cheese
salt and pepper
2 ripe dessert pears
6 lettuce leaves
1 tbsp chopped chives to garnish
paprika

Mash 1 tablespoonful yoghurt with the Cheshire cheese and refrigerate until needed. Sieve the cottage cheese into a bowl and beat in the remaining yoghurt. Season to taste. Peel, halve and core the pears and fill each cavity with a spoonful of the Cheshire cheese mixture.

Finely shred the lettuce and arrange on individual serving plates. Place a half pear, cut side down, on top. Spoon over the pear the yoghurt and cottage cheese mixture and garnish with chives and paprika.

GRAPE COCKTAIL   VV

Serves 4

175 g (6 oz) green grapes
juice of 3 medium oranges
2 tbsp lime juice cordial
mint leaves to garnish

Stone and skin the grapes, cut into small pieces and chill in the refrigerator. Cover with the orange and lime juice. Place in cocktail glasses and rechill. Garnish with a small leaf of mint just before serving.

MELON COCKTAIL   VV

Serves 4

1 small honeydew melon or 2 small
   ogen melons
a little chopped, preserved ginger
   and syrup
3 tsp white wine
1 tsp lemon juice
juice of 1 small orange
glacé cherries to decorate (optional)

Cut the melon flesh into small cubes. Mix with all the other ingredients and chill. Serve in cocktail glasses and decorate each serving with a little piece of glacé cherry.

MELON AND TOMATO VINAIGRETTE   VV

Serves 4

2 small ogen or charentais melons
4 small tomatoes
100 g (4 oz) black grapes
4 tbsp French dressing (see page
   91)
4 tbsp mint or lemon balm sprigs to
   garnish

Cut the melons in half and discard the seeds. Carefully remove the flesh; cut into cubes and reserve the shells. Skin, quarter and de-seed the tomatoes, halve and de-seed the grapes and place both in a bowl with the melon. Pour over the dressing. Mix well, then spoon the mixture into the melon shells. Chill and serve garnished with lemon balm or mint.

AVOCADO DIP

V

Serves 12

1 large ripe avocado
juice of 1 small lemon
2 tomatoes
1 clove garlic, crushed
1 small onion, grated
150 ml (¼ pint) natural yoghurt
salt and pepper

Vegetables for the dip
100 g (4 oz) button mushrooms
2 large carrots
1 small green pepper
1 small red pepper
6 celery stalks
½ small cauliflower, cut into florets

Halve the avocado and remove the stone. Mash the flesh with the lemon juice. Skin, seed and chop the tomatoes and add to the avocado with the crushed garlic, grated onion, yoghurt and seasoning to taste. Mix until smooth and place in a serving dish.

Cut the carrots, peppers and celery into fine strips. Stand the dish of avocado dip in the centre of a large plate and arrange all the vegetables in neat piles around the edge.

This is ideal for a drinks party, or, if served on individual plates, it can be used as a starter.

KIPPER PÂTÉ

Serves 6–8

225 g (8 oz) kipper fillets
1 medium lemon
100 g (4 oz) cottage cheese
freshly ground black pepper
50 g (2 oz) sunflower margarine

Cook the kipper fillets under a low grill for 5 minutes each side, then remove the skin and flake the flesh into a mixing bowl. Add the juice of 1 lemon and the cheese and mix thoroughly. Season with black pepper. Fill 6–8 ramekins with the fish mixture, smooth over the tops and chill. Melt the margarine and pour over the top. Serve with Melba toast.

This pâté will keep for several days in the refrigerator.

CHICKEN LIVER PÂTÉ

Serves 6

50 g (2 oz) streaky bacon, diced
1 small onion, diced
225 g (8 oz) chicken livers
1 clove garlic, crushed
1 bay leaf
1 sprig thyme
freshly ground black pepper
4 tbsp chicken stock
1 tbsp brandy (optional)

Put the bacon in a small saucepan with a lid and heat gently to extract a little of the fat. Add the onion and continue to cook gently until the onion is translucent but not brown. Add all the other ingredients apart from the brandy, and cook over a low heat for 15 minutes.

Remove the thyme and bayleaf. Pour the mixture into a liquidiser or food processor. Add the brandy and then process to a smooth paste. Transfer the pâté to a serving dish. Chill for at least 2 hours before serving.

TROUT MOUSSE

Serves 6 as a starter

450 g (1 lb) rainbow trout
1 stalk parsley
1 stalk fennel leaves
25 g (1 oz) sunflower margarine
salt and pepper
7 g (¼ oz) powdered gelatine
150 ml (¼ pint) water
150 ml (¼ pint) mayonnaise (see
    page 92)
150 ml (¼ pint) chicken stock
2 tbsp lemon juice
1 tsp onion juice (grate a medium
    onion and squeeze)
1 tsp Worcestershire sauce
salt and pepper
a good shake of paprika
150 ml (¼ pint) natural yoghurt
cress or parsley to garnish

Heat the oven to 180°C (350° F) mark 4. Place the trout on a sheet of foil with the parsley and fennel. Dot it with the margarine and season with salt and pepper. Close the foil securely to make a parcel and bake for 30 minutes. Leave to cool without opening the parcel.

When quite cold, flake the fish from the bone and place in a mixing bowl. Dissolve the gelatine in the water. Mix the mayonnaise, chicken stock, lemon juice, onion juice, Worcestershire sauce, salt, pepper and paprika. Add to the fish and mix carefully. Fold in the yoghurt and then the gelatine. Pour into individual ramekins and chill.

Garnish with cress or parsley and serve with wholemeal bread and butter.

MAIN COURSE DISHES

The meat and fish recipes appear at the
beginning of this chapter, followed by the
vegetarian dishes, and a selection of savoury
pancake and flan recipes.

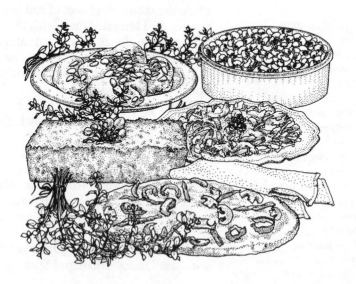

NAVARIN OF LAMB

Serves 4–6

50 g (2 oz) haricot beans
50 g (2 oz) pearl barley
900 g (2 lb) best end of neck or
shoulder of lamb
2 tbsp corn or sunflower oil
1 large onion
1 tbsp plain flour
575 ml (1 pint) stock
1 tbsp tomato purée
salt and pepper
1 bouquet garni
12 small button onions
2 small turnips
12 small carrots
2 tbsp chopped parsley to garnish

Cover the haricot beans and pearl barley with cold water and leave to soak overnight (or see alternative methods page 13). Heat the oven to 180°C (350°F) mark 4. Cut any excess fat off the meat and divide into 8 pieces.

Heat the oil in a large flameproof casserole; add the meat and fry until it is brown on all sides, then remove from the casserole. Cut the large onion into rings and fry in the casserole until golden brown. Stir in the flour, mixing well, then gradually add the stock, stirring constantly.

Add the tomato purée, salt and pepper, then return the meat to the casserole. Bring to the boil and simmer for 2 minutes, then add the drained beans, barley and the bouquet garni. Bring to the boil and bake in the oven for 1 hour.

While the meat is cooking, sauté the small onions in 1 tablespoonful oil until lightly browned. Cut the turnips into quarters and leave the carrots whole. After 1 hour, remove the bouquet garni from the casserole and add the vegetables. Continue to cook in the oven for a further 30–40 minutes until all the vegetables are tender.

Sprinkle with chopped parsley and serve immediately with jacket potatoes and a green vegetable.

LOIN OF LAMB CHOPS TARTARE

Serves 4

1 tbsp chopped gherkins or cucumber
1 tbsp capers or finely chopped onion
2 tbsp chopped parsley
4 stuffed olives, finely chopped or
   1 tsp dried rosemary
275 ml (½ pint) natural yoghurt
salt and pepper
4 large or 8 small loin of lamb chops

Heat the oven to 190°C (375° F) mark 5. Add the chopped gherkins, capers, parsley and olives or rosemary to the yoghurt; mix well and season to taste. Place the lamb chops in a shallow, ovenproof dish. Pour the yoghurt mixture over the chops and bake for about 1 hour until the lamb is tender and the yoghurt set.

Serve with pilau rice (see page 37) and a green vegetable.

PORK CHOPS BAKED IN YOGHURT

Serves 4

4 thick pork chops
2 tbsp corn or sunflower oil
175 g (6 oz) mushrooms
1 tbsp lemon juice
1 tbsp plain wholemeal flour
salt and freshly ground pepper
4 tbsp natural yoghurt
1 tbsp dried thyme or oregano
2 tbsp finely chopped fresh parsley

Heat the oven to 170°C (325° F) mark 3. Trim excess fat from the chops then sauté in the oil until brown on both sides. Remove the chops from the pan. Chop the mushrooms finely. Spoon off all but 2 tablespoonfuls oil from the pan and sauté the mushrooms until soft. Stir in the lemon juice, sprinkle with the flour and cook until slightly thickened and almost dry. Season.

Lightly oil 4 pieces of aluminium foil, each large enough to wrap a chop in. Place 1 chop on each piece of foil, divide the mushroom mixture into 4 and place a portion on top of each chop. Put 1 tablespoonful yoghurt on each chop over the mushroom mixture and sprinkle the thyme or oregano and parsley over the yoghurt.

Close and seal the foil parcels and place on a baking sheet. Cook for 45–60 minutes. Serve, still wrapped in the parcels, with baked potatoes and two other vegetables.

PORK WITH PRUNES

Serves 4

225 g (8 oz) prunes
275 ml (½ pint) red wine
700 g (1½ lb) lean shoulder or loin
  of pork or 4 pork steaks
1 tbsp plain wholemeal flour,
  seasoned with salt and pepper
2 tbsp corn or sunflower oil
1 tsp redcurrant jelly (optional)
200 ml (7 fl oz) natural yoghurt
salt and pepper
450 g (1 lb) creamed potato

Soak the prunes overnight in the wine then simmer gently in the wine for about 30 minutes. Bone and trim the pork and cut into slices 1 cm (½ inch) thick. Dust with seasoned flour and fry in the oil until brown on both sides.

Add the wine in which the prunes have been cooked and simmer gently for about 30–40 minutes. Strain. Keep the meat warm. Reduce the liquor by about one third, add the jelly if used, together with the yoghurt and seasoning. Boil quickly until thick.

Serve the slices of pork on a bed of creamed potato. Surround with the prunes and strain the sauce over the top. Serve with carrots and a green vegetable.

CHICKEN AND WHOLEWHEAT NOODLES

Serves 4

4 medium tomatoes
225 g (8 oz) onions
1 clove garlic, crushed
½ tsp dried marjoram or oregano
1.2 kg (2½ lb) roasting chicken
575 ml (1 pint) water
1 bouquet garni
225 g (8 oz) wholewheat noodles
grated Parmesan or strong Cheddar
  cheese

Heat the oven to 190°C (375°F) mark 5. Blanch, peel and slice the tomatoes. Cut the onions into rings and place them, together with the garlic, tomatoes and marjoram or oregano, in the bottom of a large, lidded, flameproof casserole. Place the chicken on top. Add the water and bouquet garni, cover and bring to the boil. Place in the oven and allow to simmer for 1 hour.

Remove the chicken from the casserole, add the noodles and cook on the hob for 10 minutes or until the pasta is just tender. Remove the chicken meat from the bone and add to the dish. Bring back to the boil and cook until the chicken is thoroughly heated through. Serve immediately with grated cheese and a green vegetable or tossed salad.

HERB BAKED CHICKEN

Serves 4

salt and freshly ground black pepper
4 chicken breasts
1 tbsp sunflower oil
2 medium onions
grated rind and juice of 1 large
  lemon
4 tbsp chopped fresh parsley or 4 tsp
  dried parsley
1 tbsp chopped fresh thyme or 1 tsp
  dried thyme
1 tbsp chopped fresh rosemary or 1
  tsp dried rosemary
1 tbsp chopped fresh mint or 1 tsp
  dried mint
150 ml (¼ pint) stock

Heat the oven to 180°C (350°F) mark 4. Season and brush the chicken breasts with the oil and bake uncovered for 30 minutes. Finely chop the onion and place in a bowl with the lemon rind and juice. Add the herbs and mix well. Season to taste.

Remove the chicken from the oven and pour off any surplus fat. Pour the stock over the chicken. Press the onion and herb mixture on top of the chicken breasts and return to the oven. Bake for 15–20 minutes until the herb topping is crisp and lightly browned. Serve hot or cold.

CHICKEN VÉRONIQUE

Serves 4

2 tsp fresh root ginger or 1½ tsp
  ground ginger
4 chicken portions
225 g (8 oz) green grapes
275 ml (½ pint) water
salt and pepper
275 ml (½ pint) natural yoghurt
1 tbsp cornflour
25 g (1 oz) toasted flaked almonds

Heat the oven to 180°C (350°F) mark 4. Peel and crush the root ginger and place with the chicken portions in an ovenproof casserole. Halve and pip the grapes and scatter them over the chicken. Add the water and seasoning. Cover the casserole and cook in the oven for 1 hour or until the chicken is tender.

Place the chicken and grapes in a warm serving dish, leaving the juices in the casserole. Pour the yoghurt into a mixing bowl, whisk in the cornflour and slowly pour the hot juices from the casserole into the yoghurt, whisking constantly. Place the mixture in a saucepan and cook on the hob over a low heat, stirring carefully, until the sauce has thickened. Season to taste.

Pour over the chicken and sprinkle the toasted almonds on top.

CHICKEN PILAFF

Serves 4

50 g (2 oz) sunflower margarine
1 medium onion
150 g (6 oz) brown rice
575 ml (1 pint) stock
450 ml (¾ pint) béchamel sauce (see
*   page 93)*
150 ml (¼ pint) red or white wine
50 g (2 oz) raisins
25 g (1 oz) almonds
salt
pinch of cinnamon
pinch of cayenne pepper
1 tbsp dried tarragon or rosemary
350 g (12 oz) cooked chicken

Using a frying pan, melt 25 g (1 oz) of the margarine. Cut the onion into rings and fry gently until soft. Remove the onion from the pan and put in the oven to keep hot. Melt the remaining margarine then add the rice, stirring until the grains are coated with fat. Gradually add the stock, stirring with a fork to keep the rice grains separate and cook for about 35 minutes, until the grains are tender. Drain if necessary and keep hot.

Meanwhile, make the béchamel sauce see page 93). Pour the wine into a saucepan and bring to the boil; remove from the heat. Add the raisins and leave covered in a warm place. Place the almonds under a grill or in a hot oven until brown.

Add the salt, cinnamon, cayenne pepper and tarragon or rosemary to the béchamel sauce. Cut the chicken into strips and add to the sauce. Bring to the boil and cook until the chicken is heated through.

Place the chicken in the sauce in the centre of a platter and surround with rice. Garnish round the edges with onion rings, toasted almonds and wine-soaked raisins.

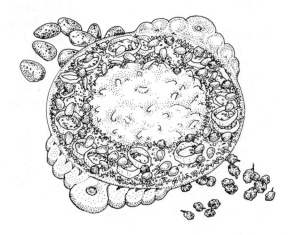

TURKEY IN HAZELNUT SAUCE

Serves 6

700 g (1½ lb) turkey breast meat
75 g (3 oz) sunflower margarine
salt and pepper
2 sprigs parsley
1 tsp fresh tarragon or rosemary
275 ml (½ pint) milk
25 g (1 oz) plain wholemeal flour
4 tbsp dry sherry
50 g (2 oz) hazelnuts, finely
  chopped
150 ml (¼ pint) double cream
paprika
chopped parsley to garnish

If the turkey is bought frozen, make sure it is thoroughly thawed. Heat the oven to 180°C (350°F) mark 4. Dot the turkey meat with 50 g (2 oz) of the margarine and season well. Add the herbs, wrap in foil and bake for 1¼ hours. Remove from the oven and cool slightly.

Place the milk, flour and the remaining margarine in a saucepan. Whisk over a moderate heat until the sauce thickens. Add the sherry and hazelnuts to the sauce. Wet a piece of greaseproof paper under the cold tap and wring out, then place directly on the surface of the sauce to prevent a skin forming.

Slice the turkey and place on a serving dish. Add the cream and the juices from the cooked turkey, to the sauce. Adjust the seasoning, bring to the boil and pour the sauce over the turkey. Return to the oven for 10–15 minutes to heat through. Garnish with paprika and parsley.

BEEF AND BEAN CASSEROLE

Serves 4–6

900 g (2 lb) braising steak
3 tbsp plain wholemeal flour,
  seasoned
3 tbsp sunflower oil
1 large onion
450 ml (¾ pint) beef stock
100 g (4 oz) haricot beans, soaked
  overnight
8 juniper berries (optional)
1 bay leaf
thinly pared rind of 1 small orange
salt and freshly ground black pepper
chopped parsley or chives to garnish

Trim all the fat from the meat and cut into large, fork-size pieces. Toss the meat in seasoned flour until well coated. Heat the oil in a flameproof casserole and fry the meat, then remove from the casserole.

Peel and slice the onion, then fry in the casserole until soft. Return the meat to the casserole and add the stock, beans and juniper berries if used. Add the bay leaf, orange rind and salt and pepper to taste, then bring to boil.

Cover the casserole and either cook in a preheated oven at 180°C (350°F) mark 4, for 2–2½ hours, or simmer on top of the stove for 2–2½ hours. Stir occasionally and add more stock if necessary. Discard the orange rind, bay leaf and juniper berries, adjust the seasoning and serve garnished with chopped parsley or chives.

A slow cooker can be used for this recipe, but the mixture must be allowed to *boil* gently for at least 20 minutes before slow cooking starts.

SAVOURY LIVER

Serves 4

450 g (1 lb) lamb's liver
2 tbsp wholewheat flour
salt and pepper
2 tbsp corn or sunflower oil
2 medium onions
150 ml (¼ pint) stock
150 ml (¼ pint) red wine
2 tbsp tomato purée
1 tsp chopped fresh thyme
1 tsp chopped fresh oregano
2 tomatoes
1 small green pepper (optional)
chopped parsley to garnish

Slice the liver and soak in salt water made up with 1 teaspoonful salt per 575 ml (1 pint) water for 15 minutes. Rinse and dry. Season the flour with salt and pepper and place in a plastic bag. Toss the liver in the flour until coated. Heat the oil in a large, flameproof casserole or frying pan and fry the liver for 2 minutes each side. Remove from the pan and keep hot.

Slice the onions and fry in the pan until soft. Stir in the stock, wine, tomato purée, thyme and oregano. Bring to the boil. Return the liver to the pan, cover and simmer for 15 minutes.

Skin, seed and slice the tomatoes and de-seed and slice the pepper if used. Add both to the pan. Cook for a further 5 minutes or until the liver is tender. Arrange on a warmed serving dish. Pour over the sauce and sprinkle with parsley.

Serve with jacket potatoes and a green vegetable or tossed salad.

LAMB CUTLETS AND PEPPER SAUCE

Serves 4

8 lamb cutlets
salt and black pepper
1 large or 2 small eggs
8 tbsp dried wholemeal breadcrumbs
150 ml (¼ pint) corn or sunflower oil
sprigs of parsley to garnish

Pepper sauce
1 large onion
2 tbsp corn or sunflower oil
4 tomatoes
1 green pepper
1 red pepper
1 clove garlic, crushed
1 tsp tomato purée
1 tsp chopped fresh marjoram,
    oregano or thyme
salt and pepper

Trim the cutlets and season with salt and pepper. Beat the eggs then coat the cutlets in the egg and breadcrumbs, passing them through the egg and crumbs twice if possible.

To make the sauce, thinly slice the onion; heat 2 tablespoonfuls oil in a pan and fry the onion until soft. Skin the tomatoes, cut into eighths and add to the pan. Core, seed and slice the peppers and add to pan (blanch them beforehand if preferred). Add the remaining ingredients, then cover and simmer for 10 minutes.

Pour about 150 ml (¼ pint) oil into a frying pan to a depth of 5 mm (¼ inch) and place over a moderate heat. When the oil is hot, add the chops and fry for 5 minutes on each side until tender and golden then drain on a wire rack over a baking tray.

Arrange the cutlets around the edge of a large serving dish and place the sauce in the centre. Garnish with sprigs of parsley and serve with noodles or jacket potatoes.

BEEF WITH MACARONI

Serves 4

225 g (8 oz) rump steak
3 tbsp sunflower or olive oil
1 small onion, finely chopped
2 cloves garlic, finely chopped
1 large aubergine, coarsely grated
200–225 g (7–8 oz) canned
   tomatoes
1 tbsp red wine
1 tbsp tomato purée
pinch of dried oregano
salt and pepper
225 (8 oz) short wholewheat
   macaroni
1 egg, beaten
15 g (½ oz) butter
½ tbsp Parmesan cheese, grated

Cut the meat into 2 cm (¾ inch) cubes. Heat the oil in a saucepan, add the onion and garlic and cook over a low heat and add the aubergine, stirring until the oil has been absorbed. Rub a separate heavy frying pan with a smear of oil, place on a high heat and fry the meat until it is well browned.

Add the meat to the onion and aubergine then stir in the tomatoes, wine, tomato purée and oregano. Season with salt and pepper and cook over a medium heat, uncovered, stirring occasionally, for about 30 minutes until the sauce is reduced and the meat tender.

Bring a large saucepan of water to the boil and put in the macaroni. Stir well and boil for about 15–20 minutes until the macaroni is just tender. Beat the egg and mix the Parmesan cheese into it. As soon as the macaroni is cooked, drain it well and place in a serving dish. Add the butter, egg and Parmesan cheese, and seasoning; toss thoroughly. Pour over the meat sauce and toss again, then serve at once.

SAUTÉ OF KIDNEYS TURBIGO

Serves 4

12–18 small pickling onions
100 g (4 oz) button mushrooms
5 lamb's kidneys
2 tbsp corn or sunflower oil
100 g (4 oz) chipolata sausages
2 tsp plain wholemeal flour
1 tsp tomato purée
1 tbsp sherry
200 ml (7 fl oz) brown stock
salt and pepper
1 bay leaf
2 slices wholemeal bread
parsley to garnish

Blanch the onions and drain. Cut the mushrooms into quarters and set aside. Skin the kidneys and cut in half lengthways and remove the core. Soak (see recipe below). Heat the oil in a casserole or deep frying pan and sauté the kidneys briskly until well browned. Remove the kidneys, lower the heat and fry the chipolatas until brown, then remove from the pan.

Add the onions and mushrooms and shake over a brisk heat for 2–3 minutes, then draw aside. Stir in the flour, purée, sherry and stock. Bring to the boil and season. Slice the sausages diagonally into 2–3 pieces and add to pan with the bayleaf and kidneys. Cover and simmer for 20–25 minutes.

To make the croûtons, either cut the bread into small triangles and fry carefully in shallow fat, or toast slices of bread, then cut into triangles.

Surround the kidney mixture with croûtons and garnish with parsley.

HEARTS IN CIDER

Serves 4

4 lamb's hearts
juice of 1 lemon
225 g (8 oz) onions
2 medium cooking apples
2–3 tbsp plain wholemeal flour
2 tbsp corn or sunflower oil
salt and freshly ground black pepper
2 bay leaves
150 ml (¼ pint) dry cider

Heat the oven to 150°C (300°F) mark 2. Remove the fat and cut the hearts into 1-cm (½-inch) slices. Soak in salt water made up with 1 teaspoonful salt per 575 ml (1 pint) water for 10 minutes, then rinse, dry and leave in the lemon juice for 30 minutes.

Peel and slice the onions; peel, quarter and slice the apples. Dry the heart slices and coat with the flour; fry in the oil in a flameproof casserole over a fairly high heat. Add the onion and continue frying until

1 tsp crushed coriander seeds or
   finely chopped fresh thyme or
   rosemary
2 thin slices unpeeled lemon

pale golden. Season with salt and freshly
ground black pepper.

Add the bay leaves and cider. Cover the
heart slices with apple, sprinkle with
coriander or herbs. Lay the slices of lemon
and the bay leaves on top of the apple slices.
Cover and simmer over a low heat on top of
the cooker or in an oven for about 1 hour,
until tender.

Remove the lemon slices and bay leaves
and stir the apple slices into the sauce. Serve
with jacket or creamed potatoes.

PORK GOULASH

Serves 4

450 g (1 lb) boned hand or shoulder
   of pork
4 tomatoes
1 tbsp corn or sunflower oil
350 g (12 oz) onions
2 tbsp plain wholemeal flour
1 tbsp paprika
575 ml (1 pint) chicken stock
2 tbsp tomato purée
grated rind of 1 lemon
salt and pepper
1 green pepper or 100 g (4 oz)
   button mushrooms
150 ml (¼ pint) natural yoghurt

Heat the oven to 180°C (350° F) mark 4. Cut
the pork into 5-cm (2-inch) cubes. Blanch,
peel and quarter the tomatoes. Heat the oil
in a flameproof casserole; slice the onions
and fry for 3 minutes stirring constantly.
Add the pork and fry until the cubes are
well browned.

Stir in 1 tablespoonful of the flour and the
paprika and cook for 1 minute, stirring
continuously. Add the chicken stock,
tomatoes, tomato purée, lemon rind, salt
and pepper. Bring to the boil, then cover
and cook in the oven for 1¼–1½ hours until
the meat is tender.

Blanch and de-seed the pepper and cut
into strips, or cut the mushrooms into
strips. Add to the casserole and cook for
another 5 minutes.

Warm the yoghurt in a small saucepan
but do not allow to boil. Add to the goulash.
Pour into a warmed serving dish, sprinkle
with more paprika and serve with jacket
potatoes.

HADDOCK AU GRATIN

Serves 4

350 g (12 oz) haddock fillet
275 ml (½ pint) water
6 tbsp white wine
1 slice onion
1 slice carrot
6 peppercorns
1 bay leaf
100 g (4 oz) button mushrooms
50 g (2 oz) sunflower margarine
50 g (2 oz) plain wholemeal flour
50 g (2 oz) strong Cheddar cheese
salt and freshly ground black pepper
25 g (1 oz) fresh wholemeal
*   breadcrumbs*

Heat the oven to 200°C (400° F) mark 6. Place the fish, water, wine, onion, carrot, peppercorns and bay leaf in a shallow, ovenproof dish. Cover with greased greaseproof paper and place in the centre of the oven. Cook for 15–20 minutes. Strain off the liquid and reserve. Flake the fish, discarding the skin, bones, the bay leaf and peppercorns. Place the flaked fish in a shallow, greased ovenproof dish.

Sauté the mushrooms in the margarine for 2–3 minutes. Stir in the flour and cook gently for another minute. Remove from the heat and gradually stir in the strained cooking liquor. Bring to the boil and continue to stir until the sauce thickens. Grate the cheese and add half of it to the sauce; season to taste.

Pour over the fish and sprinkle the remaining cheese and breadcrumbs over. Bake for 20 minutes until golden brown. Serve hot with jacket potatoes and a green vegetable.

FISH STEAKS WITH FENNEL

Serves 4

1 large fennel bulb
1 tbsp sunflower oil
225 g (8 oz) ripe tomatoes
grated rind and juice of ½ lemon
1 tbsp chopped parsley
½ tsp ground coriander
salt and pepper
4 haddock or cod steaks

Heat the oven to 180°C (350° F) mark 4. Thinly slice the fennel and fry in the oil in a medium saucepan until lightly coloured. Peel and chop the tomatoes and stir in, together with the lemon rind and juice, parsley, coriander and seasoning. Bring the mixture to the boil, stirring carefully. Cover the pan; reduce the heat and simmer for 10 minutes, stirring occasionally.

Transfer the sauce to a shallow, ovenproof dish and arrange the fish steaks on top. Cover with greased foil or greased greaseproof paper and bake for 20 minutes or until the fish is cooked through. Serve with potatoes and peas.

FISH KEBABS

Serves 4

8 small pickling onions
1 small green pepper
1 small red pepper
450 g (1 lb) white fish e.g. halibut, haddock or monkfish
8 button mushrooms
8 small tomatoes (whole but skinned)
4 tbsp corn or sunflower oil

Cook the onions in boiling water for 5 minutes. Drain, cool and halve. Blanch the peppers if liked and cut in 2.5-cm (1-inch) squares.
   Cut the fish into 2.5-cm (1-inch) cubes. Put the fish, onions, peppers, mushrooms and tomatoes on kebab skewers starting and ending with tomatoes. Season and brush with oil. Preheat the grill on high. Turn down the heat and cook for 6–8 minutes; turn and brush with oil and continue cooking for another 6–8 minutes. Serve with pilau rice (see below).

PILAU   VV

Serves 4

250 g (8 oz) long-grain brown rice
1 tbsp corn or sunflower oil
100 g (4 oz) peas
1 large onion, finely sliced
50 g (2 oz) raisins
50 g (2 oz) whole peanuts
salt and pepper

Cook the brown rice in fast boiling water for about 40 minutes and refresh in cold water. Cook the peas. In the meantime, fry the finely sliced onion rings in the oil until soft and just beginning to colour. Add the cooked rice, seasoning and other ingredients and heat through gently.

BAKED HADDOCK STEAKS

Serves 4

225 g (8 oz) button mushrooms
salt and freshly ground black pepper
4 haddock steaks
275 ml (½ pint) natural yoghurt
2 tbsp fresh chopped parsley
parsley sprigs to garnish

Heat the oven to 180°C (350° F) mark 4. Wash the mushrooms and, if large, cut into quarters. Place in a shallow greased ovenproof dish and season with salt and pepper. Place the fish steaks on top. Whisk the yoghurt until it is smooth; spread it over the haddock and sprinkle with chopped parsley. Cover with greased foil and bake for 30 minutes or until the fish is cooked through.

Serve garnished with parsley sprigs and accompany with baked tomatoes and a potato dish.

LENTIL ROAST   (VV)

Serves 4

100 g (4 oz) lentils
1 medium onion
25 g (1 oz) Cheddar cheese
1 tbsp chopped fresh parsley
1 tsp dried mixed herbs
15 g (½ oz) sunflower margarine
1 egg yolk
25 g (1 oz) wholemeal breadcrumbs
salt and pepper
2 tbsp sunflower oil

Heat the oven to 190°C (375° F) mark 5. Wash the lentils and soak overnight in 575 ml (1 pint) water (for alternative methods see page 13). Chop the onion finely and add to the lentils in the water and cook for about 30 minutes until tender and all the water has been absorbed. Stir occasionally to prevent burning.

Grate the cheese finely and add to the lentils together with the herbs, margarine, egg yolk and breadcrumbs and beat well. Add salt and pepper. Heat the sunflower oil and pour into a baking tray. Form the mixture into 2 rolls and place in the tray. Baste, then bake in the centre of the oven for about 1 hour.

Serve with 275 ml (½ pint) tomato sauce (see page 93).

For vegans, substitute 1 teaspoonful yeast extract dissolved in 150 ml (¼ pint) water for the egg yolk and cheese.

CASHEW ROAST (VV)

Serves 4

1 medium onion
1 small green pepper
1 clove garlic, crushed
1 tbsp corn or sunflower oil
1 tbsp plain flour
150 ml (¼ pint) stock or water
1–2 tbsp Shoyu soy sauce
2 tsp chopped fresh oregano or
  marjoram or ½ tsp dried oregano
  or marjoram
2 tsp chopped fresh sage or ½ tsp
  dried sage
175 g (6 oz) cashew nuts, ground
175 g (6 oz) sunflower seeds
100 g (4 oz) wholemeal
  breadcrumbs
1 egg or 2 extra tbsp water if
  necessary

Heat the oven to 190C (375° F) mark 5. Finely chop the onion and pepper. Heat the oil in a medium saucepan and sauté the onion, pepper and garlic together. Make a paste with the flour, water or stock and Shoyu soy sauce, and add to the vegetables.

Stir for a few minutes, then add all the other ingredients. If the mixture is too dry, add a beaten egg or extra water. Grease a 900-g (2-lb) loaf tin and line with greased greaseproof paper. Pour in the mixture and bake for 45 minutes.

Serve with salad and jacket potatoes.

For a vegan dish, use water or vegetable stock instead of the stock and the egg.

BRAZIL NUT PATTIES (VV)

Serves 4

225 g (8 oz) shelled Brazil nuts
50 g (2 oz) fresh wholewheat
  breadcrumbs
1 tbsp chopped fresh thyme or 1 tsp
  dried thyme
salt and pepper
1 egg

Heat the oven to 200°C (400° F) mark 6. Grind the Brazil nuts coarsely in a liquidiser or chop very finely and place in a mixing bowl. Add the breadcrumbs, thyme, salt and pepper and mix well. Beat the egg and stir it into the mixture.

Divide the mixture into 4 and shape into cakes 1 cm (½ inch) thick and 7.5 cm (3 inches) in diameter. Place the patties on a lightly greased baking sheet and bake for 20 minutes.

Serve hot or cold with jacket potatoes and a tossed salad or tomato sauce (see page 93).

For vegans, substitute 2 tablespoonfuls Shoyu soy sauce for the egg.

CHEESE, TOMATO AND WALNUT LOAF   V

Serves 4

225 g (8 oz) shelled walnuts
225 g (8 oz) tomatoes
100 g (4 oz) Lancashire or Cheddar
  cheese
1 medium onion
1 tbsp chopped fresh marjoram or
  oregano or 1 tsp dried marjoram or
  oregano
salt and pepper
1 egg
cress or watercress to garnish

Heat the oven to 200°C (400°F) mark 6. Grease a 450-g (1-lb) loaf tin. Grind the walnuts in a liquidiser or food processor, or chop finely and place in a large mixing bowl.

Peel and thinly slice the tomatoes and add to the bowl. Finely grate the cheese and onion and add, together with the herbs and seasoning. Mix well. Beat the egg and stir in. Spoon the mixture into the loaf tin and press down well. Bake for 30–40 minutes or until brown on top.

Cool the loaf in the tin and turn out on to a serving dish. Garnish with cress or watercress and serve with a green salad and jacket potatoes.

MUSHROOM AND NUT LOAF   (VV)

Serves 4

225 g (8 oz) onions
225 g (8 oz) mushrooms
225 g (8 oz) shelled Brazil nuts
2 tbsp corn or sunflower oil
100 g (4 oz) fresh wholewheat
  breadcrumbs
1 egg
1 tbsp chopped fresh parsley
2 tbsp Worcestershire sauce
seasoning

Heat the oven to 180°C (350°F) mark 4. Grease and line with foil a 450-g (1-lb) loaf tin. Dice the onions, slice the mushrooms and grind the Brazil nuts coarsely in a liquidiser or food processor or chop finely.

Heat the oil in a large saucepan. Add the onions and fry for 5 minutes stirring frequently. Add the mushrooms and fry for a further 2 minutes. Remove the pan from the heat and stir in the Brazil nuts and breadcrumbs.

Beat the egg with the parsley, Worcestershire sauce and seasoning and add to the nut mixture. Mix thoroughly, then press the mixture into the tin. Bake for 1 hour until the loaf is light brown. Turn out of the tin and serve hot with tomato sauce (see page 93) and jacket potatoes, or leave in the tin to cool, turn out and serve with salad.

For a vegan dish use 2 tablespoonfuls water instead of the egg.

ADUKI BEAN CASSEROLE   (VV)

Serves 4

350 g (12 oz) aduki beans
2 carrots
2 celery stalks
2 onions
2 tbsp sunflower or corn oil
2 cloves garlic, crushed
450 g (1 lb) bacon
450 g (1 lb) tomatoes
1 tsp tomato purée
1 bay leaf
freshly ground black pepper
chopped fresh parsley to garnish

Soak the beans overnight (or see alternative methods page 13). Drain the beans, place in a pan and cover with cold water. Bring to the boil and simmer slowly for 1 hour. Heat the oven to 180°C (350°F) mark 4. Drain and reserve 425 ml (¾ pint) of the liquid. Cut the carrots into finger pieces, and slice the celery. Slice the onions.

Heat the oil in a flameproof casserole and fry the onions for about 10 minutes until translucent. Add the carrots, celery and garlic and fry for a further 4 minutes. Dice the bacon and skin and chop the tomatoes; add both to the casserole, together with the tomato purée, bay leaf, beans and cooking liquor. Season with black pepper.

Cover and cook in the oven for 1½ hours until the beans are soft. Sprinkle with chopped parsley and serve immediately with jacket potatoes and green salad.

For a vegan dish, omit the bacon.

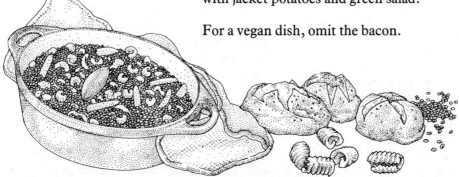

SAUSAGE AND BEAN CASSEROLE (VV)

Serves 4

350 g (12 oz) black-eyed beans
2 carrots
2 celery stalks
2 onions
2 garlic cloves, crushed
2 tbsp corn or sunflower oil
450 g (1 lb) tomatoes
450 g (1 lb) pork sausages
1 tbsp tomato purée
1 bouquet garni
freshly ground black pepper
salt
1 tbsp chopped fresh parsley or
    chives to garnish

Soak the beans overnight (or see alternative methods page 13). Drain the beans, place in a pan and cover with cold water. Bring to the boil and simmer gently for 1 hour. Drain and reserve 425 ml (¾ pint) of the liquor. Heat the oven to 180°C (350°F) mark 4.

Cut the carrots into strips and dice the celery. Slice the onions and fry in the oil in a flameproof casserole for 10 minutes until translucent but not brown. Add the carrots, celery and garlic and fry for a further 5 minutes. Skin and chop the tomatoes and add together with the sausages, tomato purée, bouquet garni, beans, reserved liquor and freshly ground pepper and salt.

Cover and cook in the oven for 1½ hours until the beans are soft. Sprinkle with parsley or chives and serve with jacket potatoes and a green salad.

For a vegan dish, omit the sausages.

CURRIED EGGS (VV)

Serves 4

4 eggs
25 g (1 oz) desiccated coconut
275 ml (½ pint) water
1 medium onion
1 small cooking apple
2 tbsp sunflower or corn oil
2 tsp curry powder
1 tbsp plain flour
1 tsp black treacle
1 tsp fruit chutney
2 tsp lemon juice
½ tsp salt

Boil the eggs for 10 minutes then plunge into cold water to prevent a black ring forming between the yolk and the white. Mix the coconut with the water in a saucepan and bring to the boil. Remove from the heat immediately and leave the saucepan, with the lid on, in a warm place for at least 10 minutes. Strain, squeeze out the coconut and reserve the liquid.

Chop the onion finely and the apple fairly coarsely. Fry the onion in the oil until it starts to soften. Stir in the curry powder and cook for a few minutes, then stir in the flour, add the coconut liquid and apple and stir the sauce until it is simmering. Add the treacle, chutney, lemon juice and salt and simmer for 1 hour.

Shell the eggs and cut in half lengthways. Drop into the sauce to heat through. Place in a hot serving dish. Serve with grapefruit segments, sliced tomato and sliced onion rings, chutney, salted nuts and poppadams each in individual bowls.

For a vegan recipe, add cooked cauliflower or courgettes to the sauce instead of the eggs.

EGGS FLORENTINE   V

Serves 4

450 g (1 lb) spinach
25 g (1 oz) sunflower margarine
salt
275 ml (½ pint) natural yoghurt
1 egg yolk
1 tsp French mustard
1 tbsp plain wholemeal flour
3 tbsp strong Cheddar cheese, grated
grated nutmeg
pepper
4 eggs

Wash the spinach thoroughly in cold water and drain. Heat the margarine in a saucepan, add the spinach and a pinch of salt. Cover the pan and sauté the spinach for about 10 minutes. (The water on the leaves and the margarine should provide enough moisture.) Drain the spinach and chop coarsely. Place in a flat, ovenproof dish and keep warm.

In a small saucepan, combine the yoghurt, egg yolk, mustard, flour and 2 tablespoonfuls of the cheese, and season with nutmeg, salt and pepper. Heat gently, stirring, until the sauce boils and thickens. Remove from the heat.

Poach the eggs and place on top of the spinach. Pour the sauce over, sprinkle with the remaining cheese and place under a hot grill until lightly browned and bubbling. Serve immediately.

PIPERADE   V

Serves 4

2 large onions
1 large red pepper
1 large green pepper
6 medium tomatoes
3 tbsp sunflower or corn oil
3 cloves garlic, crushed
salt and pepper
6 eggs
3 tbsp milk

Slice the onions into rings. Core, seed and slice the red and green peppers (blanch them as well if preferred). Skin and chop the tomatoes. Heat the oil in a fairly large frying pan, add the onion rings and fry until soft. Add the peppers, garlic, tomatoes and seasoning to taste. Simmer for 5 minutes. Beat the eggs with milk; pour into the pan and cook for a further 5 minutes, stirring occasionally.

Turn onto a heated dish and serve immediately with wholemeal bread and a tossed green salad.

MACARONI CARBONARA   (V)

Serves 4

225 g (8 oz) wholewheat macaroni
100 g (4 oz) bacon, diced
25 g (1 oz) sunflower or corn oil
4 eggs
salt and pepper
50 g (2 oz) Parmesan or strong
   Cheddar cheese, finely grated
fresh chopped parsley to garnish

Cook the macaroni in a large pan of fast boiling water until tender, then drain well. In a large pan, fry the diced bacon in oil until crisp. Add the macaroni and toss to mix well with the bacon.

In a bowl, beat the eggs with salt and pepper and pour over the pasta. Cook over a low heat, stirring carefully until the eggs start to thicken. Stir in the grated cheese and check the seasoning. Place on a warmed dish and serve garnished with chopped parsley.

For a vegetarian dish, omit the bacon and add 100 g (4 oz) chopped Brazil nuts.

CHEESE SOUFFLÉ   V

Serves 4

275 ml (½ pint) milk
50 g (2 oz) plain wholemeal flour
50 g (2 oz) sunflower margarine
100 g (4 oz) Cheddar cheese
1 tsp made mustard
½ tsp salt
¼ tsp Worcestershire sauce
3 large eggs, separated

Heat the oven to 190°C (375° F) mark 5. Place the milk, flour and margarine in a saucepan and whisk over a moderate heat until the sauce thickens, then simmer for 2 minutes. (This sauce is very thick and is known as a *panada*.) Remove from the heat and cool slightly.

Grate the cheese finely and beat in together with the mustard, salt, Worcestershire sauce and lastly the egg yolks. Beat the egg whites to stiff peaks. Gently fold into the sauce mixture with a large metal spoon. Place in a well-greased 1.5-litre (2½-pint) soufflé dish.

Place in the centre of the oven and bake for 45 minutes until the soufflé is well risen with a high, golden top. Remove from the oven and serve immediately with salad.

Variations
(1) To make mushroom soufflé, replace the cheese and Worcestershire sauce with 100 g (4 oz) finely chopped, fried mushrooms.
(2) To make onion soufflé, replace the cheese and Worcestershire sauce with 100 g (4 oz) finely chopped, boiled onions and 1 teaspoonful scissor-snipped chives.

EGGS FROM PROVENCE   V

Serves 4

1 large onion
1 clove garlic, crushed
1 tbsp sunflower or corn oil
450 g (1 lb) tomatoes
1 tsp chopped fresh oregano or
*   marjoram or ½ tsp dried oregano*
*   or marjoram*
1 tsp chopped fresh basil or ½ tsp
*   dried basil*
salt and pepper
4 eggs

Heat the oven to 190°C (375° F) mark 5.
Chop the onion and fry it with the garlic in
oil in a fairly large saucepan for 4 minutes.
Peel and coarsely chop the tomatoes and
add to the pan together with the herbs and
seasoning. Cover and cook slowly for about
20 minutes or until the tomatoes are
reduced to a purée.

Divide the purée between 4 individual
ovenproof dishes and make a hollow in the
centre of each. Break one egg into each dish
and sprinkle with salt and pepper.

Bake in the oven for 10 minutes or until
the eggs are set. Serve at once with
wholemeal bread and salad.

POTATO BAKED EGGS   V

Serves 4

700 g (1½ lb) potatoes
1 large onion
1 tbsp sunflower or corn oil
2 tbsp milk
salt and pepper
ground nutmeg
4 eggs
100 g (4 oz) mature Cheddar cheese

Heat the oven to 200°C (400° F) mark 6.
Peel the potatoes and cook in water or steam
until tender. Finely chop the onion and fry
in the oil until soft and translucent. Spread
the onion over the base of a greased 850-ml
(1½-pint) ovenproof dish. Drain the
potatoes and mash with the milk, salt,
pepper and nutmeg and beat well with a
wooden spoon. Place the creamed potato
over the onions and level the surface. Make
4 hollows in the potato with the back of a
tablespoon and crack an egg into each.

Grate the cheese and sprinkle over the
eggs and potato. Bake for 20 minutes until
the eggs have set and the cheese is golden
brown.

LENTIL AND SPINACH ROULADE   V

Serves 4

1 small onion
175 g (6 oz) red lentils
1 tbsp tomato purée
1 tbsp creamed horseradish
100 g (4 oz) sunflower margarine
450 g (1 lb) spinach
275 ml (½ pint) milk
50 g (2 oz) plain wholemeal flour
2 eggs, separated
salt and freshly ground black pepper
dry breadcrumbs

Heat the oven to 200°C (400° F) mark 6.
Grease and line a 28-cm (11-inch) Swiss roll
tin. Finely chop the onion and cook with
the lentils in a large saucepan of boiling
water until tender. Drain well, return to the
pan and heat again to drive off any
remaining moisture. Add the tomato purée,
horseradish and 50 g (2 oz) of the
margarine. Liquidise in a food processor or
rub through a sieve. Season and keep on one
side.

Wash and trim the spinach, place in a
large saucepan and sprinkle with salt but do
not add any water. Cook gently for 4–5
minutes, turn into a colander and press,
then chop very finely.

Place the milk, margarine and flour in a
saucepan and whisk over a moderate heat
until the sauce thickens. Remove from the
heat; fold in the spinach and egg yolks.
Season. Whisk the egg white until stiff and
fold into the spinach mixture. Spoon into
the prepared tin, level the surface, then
bake at the top of the oven for about 20
minutes until well risen.

Turn out on to greaseproof paper
sprinkled with breadcrumbs. Remove the
greaseproof lining, then spread the lentil
purée over the surface. Roll up like a
Swiss roll, place on a serving dish and
return to the oven for 5 minutes. Serve with
a salad.

LEEK AND RICE AU GRATIN

Serves 4

450 g (1 lb) leeks
75 g (3 oz) brown rice
75 g (3 oz) sunflower margarine
50 g (2 oz) plain wholewheat flour
275 ml (½ pint) chicken stock or
  water
3 tbsp white wine
100 g (4 oz) cooked ham
salt and freshly ground black pepper
4 large tomatoes
100 g (4 oz) Cheddar cheese
40 g (1½ oz) walnuts

Heat the oven to 180°C (350°F) mark 4. Slice the leeks crosswise into 1-cm (½-inch) pieces, then wash carefully and drain. Boil the rice in a fairly large saucepan of fast-boiling water for about 30 minutes, until tender. Drain. Melt 50 g (2 oz) of the margarine in a frying pan and sauté the leeks until golden. Remove from the heat and stir in the flour, stock and wine. Boil for 3–4 minutes, stirring continuously.

Shred the ham finely and add to the sauce. Season. Skin and slice the tomatoes and arrange to line the sides of a shallow, greased, ovenproof dish. Spoon the leek mixture into the centre.

Finely grate the cheese and chop the walnuts. Mix both with the rice and spoon over the leeks. Dot with the remaining margarine and bake for about 30 minutes. Serve with baked tomatoes and a green vegetable.

RED BEANS AND TUNA AU GRATIN   (V)

Serves 4

225 g (8 oz) red kidney beans
425 ml (¾ pint) milk
1 small piece carrot
1 small piece onion
1 bay leaf
6 peppercorns
1 blade of mace
450 g (1 lb) broccoli
200 g (7 oz) tuna, drained
salt and freshly ground black pepper
40 g (1½ oz) sunflower margarine
50 g (2 oz) plain wholemeal flour
50 g (2 oz) strong Cheddar cheese

Soak the beans overnight (or see alternative methods page 13). Heat the oven to 200°C (400°F) mark 6. Put the milk, carrot, onion, bayleaf, peppercorns and mace in a saucepan, and bring slowly to the boil. Remove from the heat and leave to infuse with the lid on. Drain the beans and cook in a pan of gently boiling water for about 1½ hours until tender, then drain.

Break the broccoli into florets and cook in a little boiling water or steam until just tender. Drain and place in a shallow, greased, ovenproof dish. Flake the tuna and mix with the cooked beans and seasoning.

Pile in the centre of the dish.

To make the sauce, strain the milk into a saucepan, add the margarine and sprinkle in the flour. Whisk over a moderate heat until the sauce thickens. Season. Pour over the tuna and broccoli mixture. Sprinkle with grated cheese and bake for 15–20 minutes until golden and bubbling.

For a lacto-vegetarian recipe, replace the tuna with 100 g (4 oz) chopped hazelnuts.

CHICK PEA CURRY   VV

Serves 4–6

450 g (1 lb) chick peas, soaked
    overnight
3 tbsp sunflower oil
2 onions, chopped
2 tsp ground cumin
2 tsp chopped fresh ginger root
1 tsp chilli powder
1 tsp ground coriander
6 cardamoms, split and the seed
    removed
2 cloves garlic, crushed
450 g (1 lb) tomatoes, skinned and
    chopped or canned tomatoes
2 tbsp tomato purée
salt and pepper
1 tbsp chopped fresh coriander or
    parsley

Drain the chick peas, place in a pan and cover with cold water. Bring to the boil and simmer for 2 hours then drain and reserve the liquid. Heat the oil in a large pan, add the onions and fry until they are soft. Add the spices and garlic and cook for a further 2 minutes. Add the tomatoes, the tomato purée, the chick peas and 275 ml (½ pint) of the reserved cooking liquid. Season to taste. Cover and simmer gently for about 1 hour or until the chick peas are tender.

Sprinkle with fresh coriander or parsley. Serve as a main course with the same accompaniments as curried eggs (see page 42).

WHOLEMEAL PANCAKE BATTER V

Makes 12 small pancakes

100 g (4 oz) plain wholemeal flour
1 egg
275 ml (½ pint) milk
1 tbsp sunflower or corn oil
corn oil for frying

Place the flour in a bowl and make a well in the centre. Add the egg, mix well, then gradually stir in half the milk and the oil. Beat thoroughly until smooth. Add enough of the remaining milk to form a batter that will coat the back of a spoon.

Heat a little oil in a 15-cm (6-inch) omelette pan and pour any surplus oil into a bowl. Pour in about 1 tablespoonful batter and tilt the pan to coat the bottom evenly. Cook over a moderate heat until the underside is lightly browned all over. Turn or toss and cook for a further 10 seconds, until the second side is brown.

Stack on an upturned saucer placed on a large plate over a pan of gently simmering water and keep warm until needed.

APRICOT AND MINT PANCAKES V

Serves 4

12 wholemeal pancakes (see above)
1 recipe quantity cheese sauce (see
    page 92)
25 g (1 oz) sunflower margarine
100 g (4 oz) wholemeal
    breadcrumbs
1 medium onion
2 tsp chopped fresh parsley or 1 tsp
    dried parsley
1 tsp chopped fresh mint or ½ tsp
    dried mint
1 tsp chopped fresh rosemary or
    ½ tsp dried rosemary
75 g (3 oz) dried apricots, chopped
150 ml (¼ pint) warm water
seasoning

Make the pancakes and the cheese sauce; keep warm. Heat the oven to 190°C (375°F) mark 5. Rub the margarine into the breadcrumbs. Finely grate the onion and add to the mixture with the herbs. Blend well. Add the chopped apricots, water and seasoning.

Use the filling to stuff the pancakes, and pour the cheese sauce over the rolled pancakes. Bake for 15–20 minutes.

SMOKED HADDOCK PANCAKES

Serves 6

12 pancakes (see page 50)
450 g (1 lb) smoked haddock fillets
275 ml (½ pint) milk, plus a little
*   extra*
65 g (2½ oz) sunflower margarine
40 g (1½ oz) plain wholemeal flour
2 hard-boiled eggs, chopped
seasoning
25 g (1 oz) Parmesan or strong
*   Cheddar cheese*
chopped fresh parsley to garnish

Heat oven to 190°C (375°F) mark 5. Make the pancakes and keep warm. Place the haddock in a pan (skin side up), add the milk, cover and bring to the boil. Simmer for 5 minutes. Remove the fish from the pan, discard the skin and bones and flake the flesh. Strain the cooking liquor and make up to 275 ml (½ pint) with more milk. Place the milk in a pan with 40 g (1½ oz) of the margarine and the wholemeal flour and whisk gently over a moderate heat until the sauce thickens. Remove from the heat, add the eggs, fish and seasoning to taste.

Place a tablespoonful of filling on each pancake. Roll up and place in a shallow, greased overproof dish. Brush with the remaining melted margarine and sprinkle with the cheese. Bake at the top of the oven for 15 minutes until crisp. Garnish with parsley and serve immediately.

SAVOURY NUT PANCAKES   V

Serves 4

12 wholemeal pancakes (see page
*   50)*
1 recipe quantity tomato sauce (see
*   page 93)*
2 medium onions
25 g (1 oz) sunflower margarine
100 g (4 oz) mixed nuts, finely
*   chopped*
seasoning
1 tbsp fresh chopped parsley or 1 tsp
*   dried parsley*
1 tbsp fresh chopped thyme or 1 tsp
*   dried thyme*
1 small egg

Heat the oven to 200°C (400°F) mark 6. Make the pancakes and the tomato sauce, and keep warm. Finely chop the onions and fry them in the margarine until soft and just starting to colour. Remove from the heat.

Add the nuts, seasoning, and herbs; bind with the egg. Divide the filling equally between the pancakes. Roll up and place in a greased, ovenproof dish. Pour the sauce over and bake in the oven for 20 minutes.

ALL-IN-ONE PASTRY   VV

Makes 175 g (6 oz) pastry

75 g (3 oz) plain wholemeal flour
75 g (3 oz) white or wholemeal
  self-raising flour
100 g (4 oz) sunflower margarine
7 tsp water

Mix the flours together. Place the margarine, water, and half the flour in a mixing bowl. Cream with a fork until well mixed. Stir in the remaining flour to form a stiff dough. Turn on to a lightly floured board and knead until smooth. Roll out and use to line a 23-cm (9-inch) flan ring.

SAVOURY QUICHE   (V)

Serves 4

1 recipe quantity all-in-one pastry
  (see above)
100 g (4 oz) streaky bacon
3 eggs
150 ml (¼ pint) milk
150 ml (2 oz) strong cheese, grated
seasoning
pinch of cayenne pepper
1 tsp chopped fresh chives

Heat the oven to 200°C (400°F) mark 6. Line a flan ring with the pastry

Dice the bacon and fry in a small pan over a gentle heat. Place in the pastry case. Mix 1 whole egg plus 2 yolks with the milk, grated cheese, salt, pepper and cayenne pepper. Whisk the egg whites until stiff; fold into the milk mixture and pour the mixture into the flan case. Sprinkle with chives.

Bake at the top of the oven for 30–35 minutes until the filling has set. The oven temperature may be lowered after 20 minutes' cooking, to 150°C (300°F) mark 2, to prevent over-browning of the top.

Omit the bacon for a lacto-vegetarian dish.

ONION FLAN   V

Serves 4

1 recipe quantity all-in-one pastry
  (see opposite)
700 g (1½ lb) onions
50 g (2 oz) sunflower margarine
2 eggs
150 ml (¼ pint) natural yoghurt
75 ml (3 fl oz) milk
salt and freshly ground pepper
pinch of grated nutmeg

Heat the oven to 200°C (400° F) mark 6. Line a flan ring with the pastry (see opposite).

Slice the onions very thinly and fry gently in the margarine in a large covered frying pan for 15 minutes. Thoroughly mix together the eggs, yoghurt, milk, salt, pepper and nutmeg. Pour a little of the egg mixture into the pastry case. Add the onions and the remaining egg mixture. Bake at the top of the oven for 30 minutes until golden and well set.

PIZZA   (V)

Serves 8–12

⅓ recipe quantity brown bread
  dough (see page 78)
25 g (1 oz) sunflower margarine
1 clove garlic, crushed
1 large onion, finely chopped
200–225 g (7–8 oz) canned
  tomatoes
2 tsp dried oregano or marjoram
75 g (3 oz) cheese, grated
3 rashers streaky bacon
4 anchovy fillets
50 g (2 oz) mushrooms

Heat the oven to 230°C (450°F) mark 8. Melt the margarine in a saucepan and add the garlic and onion. Cook until soft but not browned. Add the tomatoes and herbs and simmer for 5 minutes.

Divide the bread dough in two, knead well and form into thin rounds about 25 cm (10 inches) in diameter. Place on a well-greased baking sheet.

Spread the tomato mixture on the bases, and sprinkle the grated cheese on top. Make a lattice pattern with the anchovies, bacon and mushrooms on top of the cheese.

Turn the oven down to 200°C (400°F) mark 6 and cook the pizzas on the top shelf for 15–20 minutes. Serve hot or cold. These pizzas freeze well.

Omit the bacon and anchovies for a lacto-vegetarian dish.

VEGETABLES AND SALADS

This chapter suggests many ways of creating tasty side-dishes which help balance and enhance a main course, and also add fibre to the diet.

SWEET AND SOUR BEANS (VV)

Serves 4

225 g (8 oz) dried haricot beans
175 g (6 oz) bacon
1 medium onion
225 g (8 oz) carrots
1 large cooking apple
50 g (2 oz) raisins
1 tbsp wine vinegar
salt and pepper
225 g (8 oz) white cabbage

Soak the beans overnight in 575 ml (1 pint) cold water. Drain the beans and reserve soaking water. Add enough water to bring the liquid up to 575 ml (1 pint) again, and add to the beans in a saucepan. Cover and cook the beans for about 1 hour until tender. Drain the beans and reserve the liquid.

Place the bacon in a large saucepan and heat gently until the fat runs. Dice the onion, add to the bacon and fry for 3–5 minutes, stirring constantly. Dice the carrots, slice the apples thickly and add both, together with the raisins and drained beans, to the pan. Make the reserved cooking liquor up to 575 ml (1 pint) again and add to the pan with the wine vinegar and seasoning. Cover and simmer for 20 minutes.

Finely shred the cabbage, add to the pan and continue to cook with the lid on for 5–10 minutes until the vegetables are tender. Serve hot with jacket potatoes and a tossed salad.

For a vegan dish, omit the bacon.

AUTUMN CARROTS VV

Serves 4

350 g (12 oz) carrots
225 g (8 oz) mushrooms
50 g (2 oz) sunflower margarine
seasoning
fresh chopped mixed herbs to garnish

Cut the carrots into fine julienne strips and cook in boiling water or steam for about 10 minutes. Drain. Wipe the mushrooms and cut into fairly large dice.

Heat the oil in a pan, add the carrots and cook, stirring well, for about 5 minutes. Add the mushrooms and seasoning and cook for a further 5 minutes. When the vegetables are soft, place in a warm serving dish and sprinkle with herbs.

COURGETTES WITH TOMATOES   VV

Serves 4

700 g (1½ lb) courgettes
salt
100 g (4 oz) sunflower margarine
225 g (8 oz) tomatoes
4 tbsp chopped fresh parsley
1 clove garlic, crushed
1 tsp brown sugar
freshly ground black pepper

Cut the courgettes into 1-cm (½-inch) slices and arrange on a flat platter. Sprinkle with salt and leave to stand for 1 hour. Rinse and dry well using kitchen paper. Melt 75 g (3 oz) of the margarine in a frying pan. Add the courgettes and fry gently until soft and transparent. Place in a serving dish and keep warm.

Skin and chop the tomatoes. Melt the remaining margarine and add the tomatoes, parsley, garlic, sugar and pepper to taste. Cook until the mixture forms a thickish purée. Adjust the seasoning and pour the purée over the courgettes in a serving dish.

This dish is an excellent accompaniment to roast meat.

SPICED CAULIFLOWER   V

Serves 4

2 tbsp sunflower oil
1 tsp ground ginger
2 tsp ground coriander
1 tsp ground turmeric
1 cauliflower, broken into florets
2 carrots, cut into julienne strips
1 onion, sliced
2 celery stalks, diced
150 ml (¼ pint) vegetable stock
salt and pepper
150 ml (¼ pint) natural yoghurt
fresh chopped parsley to garnish

Heat the oil in a saucepan; add the ginger, coriander and turmeric and fry gently for 1 minute. Add the cauliflower, carrots, onion and celery and cook gently for a further 4 minutes, stirring occasionally. Add the stock and seasoning to taste. Cover and simmer for 10 minutes until the vegetables are just tender. Strain, then stir in the yoghurt. Transfer to a warm serving dish. Sprinkle with parsley before serving.

LEMON AND HERB CAULIFLOWER   VV

Serves 4

1 medium cauliflower
150 ml (¼ pint) water
1 tbsp lemon juice
salt and freshly ground black pepper
1 tbsp chopped fresh chives or 1 tsp
   dried chives
1 tbsp chopped fresh parsley or 1 tsp
   dried parsley

Break the cauliflower into florets and place in a large saucepan. Boil the water, pour over the cauliflower and add the lemon juice. Sprinkle with salt and pepper. Cover the pan and simmer over a low heat for 5–10 minutes until the cauliflower is tender but still crisp.

Remove the cauliflower; place in a warmed serving dish and keep warm. Boil the cooking liquor rapidly until it is reduced to 4 tablespoonfuls. Stir in the chives and parsley. Pour the liquid over the cauliflower.

CONCOMBRE CRÉCY   VV

Serves 4

½ large cucumber
450 g (1 lb) carrots
50 g (2 oz) sunflower margarine
salt
chopped parsley to garnish

Peel the cucumber, scrape the carrots and cut both into pieces about 5 x 0.5 cm (2 x ¼ inches). Melt the margarine in a pan, add the carrots and salt and just enough water to cover. Cook until nearly tender, add the cucumber and cook for a further 7–10 minutes. The liquid will evaporate leaving the vegetables lightly coated with margarine. Garnish with chopped parsley.

BRUSSELS SPROUTS WITH ALMONDS   VV

Serves 4

450 g (1 lb) Brussels sprouts
25 g (1 oz) almonds
25 g (1 oz) sunflower margarine
freshly ground black pepper

Prepare and boil the Brussels sprouts in water or steam for about 7–10 minutes until tender but still slightly crisp. Blanch the almonds, cut into shreds then lightly brown under the grill or in a hot oven. Drain the sprouts and place in a warm serving dish. Melt the margarine, add the almonds, season with pepper and pour over the sprouts.

COURGETTES PROVENÇALE (VV)

Serves 4

4–6 baby marrows or courgettes
1 shallot
2 tbsp sunflower or corn oil
450 g (1 lb) tomatoes
75 g (3 oz) grated cheese
salt and freshly ground black pepper

Heat the oven to 190°C (375°F) mark 5. Cut the courgettes into 5-cm (2-inch) slices and chop the shallot very finely. Sauté both in hot oil for 10–15 minutes. Skin the tomatoes, cut into quarters and sauté in a separate pan.

Grease an ovenproof dish and layer up the tomatoes and courgettes alternately, with grated cheese sprinkled between each layer. End with a tomato layer sprinkled with cheese. Season with salt and pepper and cook in the oven for 45 minutes.

For a vegan dish, omit the cheese.

RATATOUILLE VV

Serves 4–6

2 large aubergines
2 medium courgettes
350 g (12 oz) ripe tomatoes
1 green pepper
1 onion
2 cloves garlic, crushed
3 tbsp olive or sunflower oil
salt and freshly ground black pepper

Slice the aubergines and the courgettes. Lay the slices flat on a plate and sprinkle with salt. Skin the tomatoes and cut into rough pieces. Halve the pepper, remove the core and seeds and shred finely. Slice the onion. Heat the oil in a saucepan, add the onion and garlic and cook for 2–3 minutes. Rinse the aubergine and the courgette slices thoroughly in water, then dry them on kitchen paper, drop into the pan and fry for 2–3 minutes on each side. Season, then add the tomatoes and peppers. Cover the pan and cook gently for at least 1 hour.

An alternative method is to transfer the mixture to a casserole after the initial frying, then continue cooking in the oven at 180°C (350°F) mark 4.

Ratatouille is often served hot, but it can be chilled and served with quarters of lemon and brown bread and butter as a starter.

DUCHESSE POTATOES   V

Serves 6

450 g (1 lb) cooked potato
25 g (1 oz) sunflower margarine
1 egg
2 tsp salt
freshly ground black pepper
good pinch of grated nutmeg
water and salt to glaze

Heat oven to 200°C (400°F) mark 6. Pass the hot potatoes through a ricer or sieve. Melt the margarine in a saucepan, add the potato and beat well; add the egg, salt, pepper and nutmeg and beat well again, adding more margarine if necessary.

Place the mixture in a forcing bag fitted with a 1-cm (½-inch) star nozzle. Pipe in pyramids on to a greased baking tray. Mix the egg with 1 tablespoonful water and ½ teaspoonful salt, and drip this on to the potatoes as a glaze. Bake at the top of the oven for about 20 minutes until brown and crisp at the edges.

POTATO CROQUETTES   V

Serves 6

450 g (1 lb) potatoes
1 egg yolk
15 g (½ oz) sunflower margarine
2 tsp finely chopped parsley
pinch of nutmeg
salt and pepper
a little plain wholemeal flour
1 egg
1 tbsp corn oil
50–75 g (2–3 oz) dried
   breadcrumbs
deep fat for frying
parsley sprigs to garnish

Peel the potatoes and boil or steam for 10–15 minutes until cooked. Drain well and dry over a gentle heat. Pass through a ricer or sieve, beat in the egg yolk, margarine, chopped parsley, nutmeg, salt and pepper.

Lightly flour a pastry board and divide the mixture into 8. Roll into barrel-shaped pieces. Mix the egg with the oil and pass the potato portions through the egg/oil and crumbs twice. Fry in deep fat using a frying basket. Fry no more than four croquettes at a time.

Serve very hot garnished with parsley.

POTATOES BADOISE   V

Serves 4

700–900 g (1½–2 lb) potatoes
2 small eggs, separated
seasoning
75 g (3 oz) cheese, grated

Heat the oven to 190°C (375°F) mark 5. Prepare and cook the potatoes, drain well and pass through a ricer or press through a sieve. Beat in the egg yolks, seasoning and cheese.

Whisk the egg whites and fold into the mixture. Spread two thirds of the mixture into a greased, ovenproof dish. Pipe the remainder on to the top. Bake at the top of the oven for 30 minutes until risen.

Duchesse potatoes, croquettes and potatoes badoise can all be prepared ahead of time and frozen until required.

APPLE, CELERY AND WALNUT SALAD   V

Serves 4–6

4 eating apples
lemon juice
1 medium head of celery
3 tbsp mayonnaise (see page 92)
50 g (2 oz) walnuts

Core and dice the apples and sprinkle with lemon juice. Finely chop the celery. Mix the apples, celery and mayonnaise in a salad bowl. Chill for 30 minutes. Chop the walnuts and stir in just before serving.

MUSHROOM SALAD   VV

Serves 4–6

2 tsp Worcestershire sauce
1 tbsp Shoyu soy sauce
salt
freshly ground black pepper
450 g (1 lb) button mushrooms
chopped fresh parsley to garnish

Mix together the Worcestershire sauce, Shoyu soy sauce, salt and pepper. Slice the mushrooms thinly and toss into the sauce mixture. Leave for 1 hour. Turn into a deep serving dish and garnish with chopped parsley.

CABBAGE AND GRAPE SALAD   VV

Serves 6

½ medium white cabbage
2 medium carrots
100 g (4 oz) green grapes
1 tsp made mustard
3 tbsp dry white wine
3 tbsp olive oil

Shred the cabbage very finely and grate the
carrots on a medium grater. Halve and seed
the grapes. Put the cabbage, carrots and
grapes in a salad bowl. Place the mustard in
a small bowl and gradually beat in the wine
and then the oil. Add the dressing to the
salad and mix thoroughly. Leave the salad
to stand for 10–15 minutes before serving.

CARROT AND WATERCRESS SALAD   VV

Serves 4

350 g (12 oz) carrots
1 bunch watercress
2 tbsp black poppy seeds
4 tbsp sunflower oil
2 tbsp cider vinegar or distilled
    vinegar
1 clove garlic, crushed
salt
freshly ground black pepper

Grate the carrots finely; chop the watercress
and mix both together. Place in a salad bowl
and stir in the poppy seeds. Mix together
the oil, vinegar, garlic and pepper and fold
into the salad.

CUCUMBER SALAD   VV

Serves 4

1 cucumber
salt

Dressing
1 tbsp clear honey
1 tbsp warm water
2 tbsp finely chopped fresh parsley
4 tbsp white wine vinegar

Slice the cucumber very thinly, arrange on a large platter, sprinkle with salt and leave for at least 30 minutes. Place the honey, water, parsley and vinegar in a screw-topped jar, shake well and leave for 30 minutes.

Carefully rinse the cucumber slices and dry on kitchen paper. Arrange the cucumber slices overlapping on a shallow dish. Shake the dressing again and pour over the cucumber. Put a plate on top and refrigerate for at least 30 minutes before serving with cold meat or fish.

CABBAGE SALAD   VV

Serves 4–6

½ small white cabbage
½ small red cabbage
50 g (2 oz) raisins
juice and finely grated rind of 1 large
   lemon
1 tbsp snipped chives or chopped
   fresh parsley

Shred the white and red cabbage very finely and place in a salad bowl with the raisins. Add the lemon juice and rind and chives or parsley. Refrigerate for 30–60 minutes before serving.

CHINESE CABBAGE SALAD   VV

Serves 4

6 leaves Chinese cabbage
2 oranges
1 bunch watercress or mustard and
   cress
3 tbsp French dressing (see page 91)
1 tbsp finely chopped fresh parsley to
   garnish

Shred the Chinese cabbage finely. Grate the orange rind finely, peel and break the orange into segments. Place the cabbage, orange, grated rind and watercress or mustard and cress in a salad bowl. Pour the dressing over, toss well and garnish with parsley before serving.

RED APPLE AND NUT SALAD   (VV)

Serves 4

4 small red apples
1 small banana
1 tbsp Brazil nuts or hazelnuts
1 bunch watercress
4 tbsp soured cream dressing (see
* page 91)*
4 lettuce leaves

Wash the apples, cut off the tops then remove the cores and scoop out the flesh leaving a thin casing. Chop the apple flesh, banana, nuts and watercress, retaining a few sprigs of watercress for garnishing. Mix the fruit, nuts and watercress with the dressing. Fill the apple cases with the dressed salad and replace the tops. Stand each apple on a lettuce leaf and garnish with sprigs of watercress.

For a vegan recipe, use 4 tablespoonfuls French dressing (see page 91) instead of the soured cream dressing.

BROWN RICE SALAD   VV

Serves 4

100 g (4 oz) long-grain brown rice
100 g (4 oz) sweetcorn
1 small red pepper
1 small green pepper
2 tsp chopped fresh chives or 4
* chopped spring onions*
25 g (1 oz) peanuts, chopped
25 g (1 oz) sultanas
4 tbsp soy sauce dressing (see page
* 92)*
2 tbsp finely chopped fresh parsley to
* garnish*

Cook the rice in fast boiling water for 35–40 minutes until tender. In a separate pan of boiling water, cook the sweetcorn for 10–15 minutes.

Core, seed, slice (and blanch if liked) the red and green peppers.

Drain the sweetcorn; rinse and drain the rice. Place the rice and sweetcorn in a bowl and mix with the peppers, chives or spring onion, peanuts and sultanas. Add the dressing, toss thoroughly and transfer to a serving dish. Sprinkle with parsley.

PUDDINGS AND SWEETS

The recipes in this chapter avoid the over-use of
heavy cream, butter and sugar; they
concentrate instead on the use of fresh fruit,
nuts, honey, low-cholesterol margarine,
yoghurt and wholemeal flour.

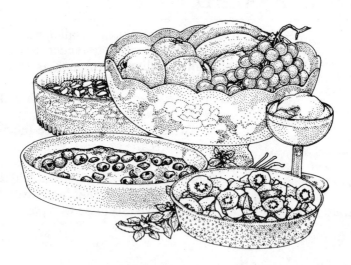

KHOSHAF (DRIED FRUIT SALAD) VV

Serves 6

100 g (4 oz) dried apricots
100 g (4 oz) seedless raisins
100 g (4 oz) dried prunes
100 g (4 oz) dried figs
575 ml (1 pint) water, mixed with 1
tbsp rose or orange flower water
50 g (2 oz) blanched flaked almonds
25 g (1 oz) pistacio nuts, split

Wash all the dried fruit and put in a large bowl. Add the water mixed with rose or orange flower water and leave to soak for at least 2 days. Just before serving, sprinkle with the nuts. Serve plain or with natural yoghurt.

Variation
Substitute the zest of 1 large orange for the rose or orange flower water, and soak in the water overnight. Strain and add to the fruit.

DANISH FRUIT TRIFLE (VV)

Serves 4

65 g (2½ oz) sunflower margarine
100 g (4 oz) fresh wholemeal
breadcrumbs
25 g (1 oz) soft brown sugar
finely grated rind of ½ lemon
225–350 g (8–12 oz) cooking
apples
225 g (8 oz) blackberries
1 tbsp water
clear honey to taste
a few extra blackberries to decorate

Melt 50 g (2 oz) of the margarine in a frying pan and fry the breadcrumbs until golden. Stir in the sugar and lemon rind and heat through, stirring constantly. Leave on one side to cool.

Peel, core and slice the apples and cook together with blackberries, water and remaining 15 g (½ oz) margarine until soft. Purée in a liquidiser or food processor, then strain through a nylon sieve. Sweeten to taste with honey, then cool. Layer up the crumb and fruit mixtures alternately in a glass bowl, finishing with a crumb layer. Decorate with extra blackberries.

Serve with whipped cream or yoghurt.

This delicious, textured sweet is ideal after a heavy main course. For vegans, serve without cream or yoghurt.

FRUIT SALAD VV

Serves 4

4 tbsp clear honey
150 ml (¼ pint) water
1 large orange
1 small lemon
1 large eating apple, cored and sliced
100 g (4 oz) black grapes, halved
    and seeded
100 g (4 oz) strawberries, sliced
1 large kiwi fruit, peeled and sliced
1 small ogen melon, diced
1 banana, peeled and sliced
a few scented geranium leaves, to
    decorate

Dissolve the honey in the water in a saucepan over a low heat. Peel the zest off the orange and lemon and add it to the syrup. Cut the pith and skin off the orange and segment it. Prepare the other fruits except the banana and put them all in a bowl. Squeeze the lemon and add the juice to the fruit, then leave the fruit on one side.

Add the orange and lemon peels and fruit cores to the syrup. Boil for 5 minutes, then strain, cool and refrigerate. When the syrup is cold, pour it over the fruit. Add the sliced banana just before serving. Serve in a large glass salad bowl or in individual dishes. Decorate with scented geranium leaves.

TRADITIONAL COOKED CHEESECAKE V

Serves 6

Base
8 digestive biscuits
25 g (1 oz) sunflower margarine,
    melted

Filling
2 eggs, separated
pinch of salt
100 g (4 oz) sunflower margarine
100 g (4 oz) soft brown sugar
a little lemon juice
2-3 drops vanilla essence
450 g (1 lb) curd cheese
1 tbsp cornflour
50 ml (2 fl oz) single cream or top of
    milk

Heat the oven to 180°C (350°F) mark 4. Process or crush the biscuits. Melt the margarine and mix with the biscuit crumbs. Spread the crumb mixture on the bottom of a greased, loose-bottomed 18-cm (7-inch) diameter cake tin.

Whisk the egg whites with the salt until stiff and leave on one side. In a separate bowl, cream together the margarine and sugar, then beat in the yolks. Add the lemon juice, vanilla essence, cheese and cornflour. Beat well, adding the cream gradually. Fold in the whisked egg whites and pour the mixture into the cake tin over the crumb mixture.

Bake for 1 hour in the centre of the oven. Turn off the heat and leave the cake in the oven until cold.

BLACKCURRANT WHIP

Serves 6

450 g (1 lb) blackcurrants
100 g (4 oz) soft brown sugar or
*   clear honey*
3 tbsp cold water
3 tsp powdered gelatine
2 tbsp kirsch or brandy (optional)
150 ml (¼ pint) natural yoghurt
3 egg whites
3 tsp chopped hazelnuts

Cook the blackcurrants gently with the sugar or honey until pulpy. Liquidise and then sieve to remove the seeds. Place the cold water in a bowl then sprinkle on the gelatine. Place the bowl over a pan of hot water until the gelatine dissolves, then stir into the fruit purée with the kirsch or brandy if used. Cool for 5–10 minutes until the mixture starts to set.

Fold in the yoghurt. Whisk the egg whites until stiff and fold into the fruit mixture. Spoon into 6 individual dishes and decorate with hazelnuts. Chill before serving.

QUORN APPLES   VV

Serves 6

3 tbsp clear honey
juice of 1 lemon
200 ml (7 fl oz) water
4 large firm dessert apples
2 large oranges
50 g (2 oz) granulated sugar
3 tbsp water

Boil the honey, lemon juice and water together to make a syrup. Peel and core the apples, cut into eighths and poach gently in the syrup. Using a potato peeler, remove the zest from one of the oranges. Cut the zest into narrow julienne strips and place in a small pan of cold water. Bring to the boil, then rinse in cold water. Cut the oranges into segments, removing all the pith and skin and add any juice to the apple syrup.

To prepare the caramel, place the sugar in a heavy-based pan with the water. Bring to the boil and boil quickly until golden brown. Pour the caramel on to an oiled tin and leave to set. When cold, break into pieces.

Place the apples in a glass bowl and arrange the orange sections on top. Scatter over the julienne strips. Just before serving, sprinkle with caramel, but don't add in advance as it will dissolve in the syrup.

LEMON DELIGHT V

Serves 4

50 g (2 oz) sunflower margarine
100 g (4 oz) soft brown sugar
2 eggs, separated
50 g (2 oz) wholemeal self-raising
   flour
finely grated rind and juice of 1
   lemon
275 ml (½ pint) milk

Heat the oven to 200°C (400°F) mark 6. Cream together the margarine and sugar until fluffy. Add the egg yolks and beat well. Fold in the flour, then fold in the lemon juice, rind and milk. Whisk the egg whites until stiff. Fold them into the lemon mixture and pour into a buttered, ovenproof dish. Stand the dish in a *bain marie* (a bowl containing enough hot water to come half way up the sides of the dish) and cook for 45–60 minutes until the top feels spongy.

STUFFED PEARS VV

Serves 4

4 large pears
50 g (2 oz) stoned dates, chopped
50 g (2 oz) blanched almonds,
   chopped
2 tbsp clear honey
150 ml (¼ pint) white wine

Heat the oven to 180°C (350°F) mark 4. Cut a thin slice from the base of each pear, so that they stand upright. Peel the pears and slice a 2.5-cm (1-inch) piece off the top of each to make a lid. Carefully scoop out the cores with a teaspoon.

Mix together the dates, almonds and honey and spoon into the hollows left in the pears. Cover with the lids then stand the pears in a greased, ovenproof dish and pour in the wine. Bake for about 30 minutes.

GRAPE SNOW V

Serves 4

450 g (1 lb) grapes
2 egg whites
275 ml (½ pint) natural yoghurt
finely grated rind of 1 orange

Skin the grapes, cut in half and remove the pips. Chop half the grapes finely, leaving the rest to one side. Whisk the egg whites stiffly and fold in the yoghurt, orange rind and chopped grapes.

Arrange the halved grapes in layers with the grape snow in individual glasses. Decorate with halved grapes.

MANDARIN CUSTARD   V

Serves 4

6 mandarin oranges
1 tbsp marmalade
275 ml (½ pint) natural yoghurt
2 eggs, separated
1 tbsp soft brown sugar

Heat the oven to 180°C (350° F) mark 4. Finely grate the rind of three of the mandarins. Divide the marmalade into four and place a portion in each of 4 ramekins or individual ovenproof dishes, or place the whole amount in one large ovenproof dish. Divide the mandarins into segments and divide between the dishes or place in the large dish.

Beat together the yoghurt, egg yolks, sugar and grated mandarin rind. Whisk the egg whites until stiff, fold into the yoghurt mixture and pour over the mandarins.

Place the dishes in a *bain marie* (a roasting tin containing enough hot water to come halfway up the sides of the dishes). Bake for 30–40 minutes until the custard is set and firm to the touch. Serve at once.

If you prefer the tops unbrowned, place foil over the top of the dishes before baking.

HOT COFFEE PUDDING   V

Serves 4

100 g (4 oz) sunflower margarine
175 g (6 oz) soft brown sugar
1 egg, beaten
3 tbsp coffee essence
100 g (4 oz) wholemeal self-raising
    flour
25 g (1 oz) walnuts, chopped
275 ml (½ pint) milk

Heat the oven to 170°C (325° F) mark 3. Cream the margarine and beat in 100 g (4 oz) of the sugar. Gradually beat in the egg and coffee essence, then lightly fold in the flour and walnuts, adding a little of the milk to give a soft, dropping consistency. Spoon into a 1-litre (2-pint) buttered, ovenproof dish. Blend together the remaining brown sugar and milk, and pour evenly over the pudding mixture. Bake for about 1½ hours in the centre of the oven until spongy to the touch.

This pudding separates to produce its own sauce but can be served with chilled yoghurt.

APPLE AND BLACKCURRANT SNOW   V

Serves 4

700 g (1½ lb) cooking apples
4 tbsp blackcurrant jelly
rind and juice of ½ lemon
150 ml (¼ pint) natural yoghurt
2 egg whites
1 tbsp water
15 g (½ oz) flaked almonds

Peel, core and slice the apples and place in a saucepan with 3 tablespoonfuls of the blackcurrant jelly and the lemon juice and rind. Cover the pan and cook over a low heat, stirring occasionally, for about 15 minutes until the apples are reduced to a pulp. Sieve the apples or purée in a food processor or liquidiser. Cool thoroughly.

Fold in the yoghurt. Whisk the egg whites until stiff and fold into the apple and yoghurt mixture. Pour into a glass serving bowl or individual dishes.

Gently heat the remaining blackcurrant jelly with the water until the jelly has dissolved. Add the flaked almonds and stir carefully until the almonds are coated. Turn onto a plate. Allow to cool thoroughly then arrange the flaked almonds on top of the apple snow.

DAMSON CHARLOTTE   (VV)

Serves 4

700 g (1½ lb) damsons
grated rind and juice of 1 lemon
175 g (6 oz) fresh wholemeal
  breadcrumbs
50 g (2 oz) soft brown sugar
50 g (2 oz) sunflower margarine

Heat the oven to 190°C (375°F) mark 5. Stone the damsons and place half of them in an overproof dish together with the juice of half the lemon. Place the breadcrumbs in a mixing bowl with the lemon rind and sugar and mix well.

Arrange half the crumb mixture on top of the damsons. Add the remaining damsons and lemon juice and then another layer of the crumb mixture. Dot the top with margarine and bake for 30–40 minutes until the topping is crisp and brown. Serve hot with natural yoghurt.

For vegans, do not serve with yoghurt.

BLACKCURRANT CLAFOUTI V

Serves 4

100 g (4 oz) strong plain white flour
pinch of salt
1 egg
275 ml (½ pint) milk
1 tbsp corn or sunflower oil
350 g (12 oz) blackcurrants

Heat the oven to 220°C (425° F) mark 7.
Sieve the flour and salt into a mixing bowl.
Make a well in the centre and break in the
egg. Work in the flour gradually from the
sides of the bowl. Add 150 ml (¼ pint) of
the milk and beat in, then beat in the
remaining milk to make a smooth batter.

Pour the oil into an ovenproof dish and
place in the oven. When the oil is hot, add
the fruit and pour the batter over the top.
Bake for 40–45 minutes until the clafouti is
well risen and brown. Serve hot.

FRUIT CRUMBLE VV

Serves 4

225 g (8 oz) cooking apples
225 g (8 oz) blackberries
1 tbsp clear honey
2 tbsp water
100 g (4 oz) plain wholemeal flour
pinch of nutmeg
50 g (2 oz) sunflower margarine
25 g (1 oz) hazelnuts or walnuts,
    finely chopped
50 g (2 oz) soft brown sugar

Heat the oven to 180°C (350° F) mark 4.
Peel, core and slice the apples and mix with
the blackberries. Place the fruit in a 1-litre
(2-pint) pie dish and add the honey and
water.

To make the crumble, mix the flour and
nutmeg together and rub in the margarine
until the mixture resembles fine
breadcrumbs. Stir in the nuts and sugar.
Spoon the crumble mixture over the fruit
and press down gently. Bake for 25–30
minutes until golden brown. Serve hot or
cold.

APPLE FLAN (VV)

Serves 4

1 large dessert apple
2 tbsp lemon juice
575 g (1¼ lb) cooking apples
25 g (1 oz) sunflower margarine
2 tbsp water
50 g (2 oz) soft brown sugar
175 g (6 oz) all-in-one sweet
　flan pastry (see below)
25 g (1 oz) icing sugar
2 tbsp apricot jam

Heat the oven to 190°C (375° F) mark 5. Wash, core and finely slice the dessert apple; pour over it 1 tablespoonful of the lemon juice and leave aside. Peel, core and slice the cooking apples. Melt the margarine in a saucepan and add the cooking apples, water and brown sugar. Cover and cook over a low heat until the apples are soft.

Turn the mixture into a basin and whisk with a fork. Pour into the flan case and arrange the slices of dessert apple in circles on top of the apple pulp. Dust with the icing sugar and bake for about 10–15 minutes.

To make the glaze, heat the apricot jam with 1 tablespoonful water and the remaining lemon juice. Remove the flan from the oven and top with the hot apricot glaze.

ALL-IN-ONE SWEET FLAN PASTRY (VV)

Makes 175 g (6 oz)

175 g (6 oz) soft plain white flour
50 g (2 oz) plain wholemeal flour
1 egg yolk
2 tbsp cold water
150 g (5 oz) sunflower margarine

Heat the oven to 200°C (400° F) mark 6. Mix the flours together. Mix the egg yolk with the water. Place half the flour mixture, egg yolk and water and the margarine in a mixing bowl and, using a fork, blend the ingredients together. Add the remaining flour and continue to mix to form a soft dough.

Roll out the pastry and line a 20–23-cm (8–9-inch) fluted flan ring or ceramic dish. Prick the bottom with a fork and place a piece of greased greaseproof paper, greased side down, over the base of the pastry. Spread ceramic balls, dried beans or rice over the paper to maintain the shape of the pastry (it is worth keeping some haricot beans or rice especially for this purpose as they can be used over and over again).

Bake the case for 10–15 minutes until the pastry is almost cooked. Remove the paper with the beans and put the flan case back in the oven for a further 5 minutes to complete the cooking. When cold, fill the case as required.

For vegans, omit the egg yolk and add 2 teaspoonfuls extra water.

RASPBERRY FLAN   V

Serves 4–6

25 g (1 oz) sunflower margarine
25 g (1 oz) plain white flour
150 ml (¼ pint) milk
25 g (1 oz) caster sugar
1 egg yolk
1 tbsp top of milk
1 tbsp sherry
175 g (6 oz) all-in-one sweet
    flan pastry (see opposite)
450 g (1 lb) fresh or frozen
    raspberries
2 tsp arrowroot
150 ml (¼ pint) water
25 g (1 oz) granulated sugar
2 tbsp lemon juice and 2 strips lemon
    zest
2 tsp raspberry jam

To prepare the custard, whisk the margarine, flour and milk in a saucepan over a moderate heat until it boils, then continue cooking for 2–3 minutes whisking continuously. Remove from the heat and leave to cool. Whisk in the caster sugar, egg yolk, top of milk and sherry, then spread the custard over the base of the flan case. Arrange the raspberries over the top of the custard.

For the glaze, mix the arrowroot with a little of the water until well blended, then place in a small saucepan together with the granulated sugar, lemon juice and zest and raspberry jam. Bring to the boil, stirring continuously, and cook for 1–2 minutes until it is clear. Strain through a nylon sieve and spread over the raspberries. Leave to cool.

BAKING WITH WHOLE GRAINS

This chapter includes two crunchy breakfast
cereals and a selection of wholemeal breads,
cakes, biscuits and tea loaves, some containing
nuts, dried fruit and oats.

CRUNCHY BREAKFAST CEREAL VV

Makes about 2.3 g (5 lb)

900 g (2 lb) rolled oats
175 g (6 oz) wheatgerm
50 g (2 oz) slivered almonds
50 g (2 oz) cashew nuts, chopped
75 g (3 oz) miller's bran
175 g (6 oz) shredded coconut
50 g (2 oz) sunflower seeds
275 ml (½ pint) sunflower oil
450 g (1 lb) clear honey
150 ml (¼ pint) water
¼ tsp vanilla essence

Heat the oven to 130°C (250°F) mark 1.
Mix all the dry ingredients in a large bowl.
Blend the sunflower oil, honey, water and
vanilla essence in a large saucepan; warm
slightly and pour over the dry ingredients.
Stir thoroughly and spread on to Swiss roll
tins. Bake for 1½–2 hours stirring
occasionally. Turn off the heat and leave the
mixture to cool in the oven.

Store in screw-topped jars.

MUESLI VV

Makes about 1.4 kg (3¼ lb)

225 g (8 oz) rolled oats
225 g (8 oz) bran flakes
225 oz (8 oz) bran
100 g (4 oz) wheatgerm
100 g (4 oz) dried apricots, finely
   chopped
100 g (4 oz) sultanas
100 g (4 oz) raisins
100 g (4 oz) currants
100 g (4 oz) sunflower seeds
100 g (4 oz) hazelnuts, almonds or
   walnuts, chopped

Mix all the ingredients in a large mixing
bowl and store in a screw-topped jar. Serve
with yoghurt and milk or fresh orange juice.

The mixture makes a delicious breakfast
dish that will keep for up to a month.

WALNUT AND BANANA CRUNCH V

Makes 16 slices

100 g (4 oz) corn or sunflower
  margarine
100 g (4 oz) molasses sugar
2 eggs
100 g (4 oz) wholemeal self-raising
  flour
2 bananas, mashed
75 g (3 oz) walnuts, chopped

Heat the oven to 190°C (375° F) mark 5. Grease and line a 20-cm (8-inch) square shallow tin. Cream the margarine and sugar together until light and fluffy. Beat in the eggs one at a time, adding a teaspoonful of flour with the second egg. Fold in the remaining flour, bananas and 50 g (2 oz) of the nuts.

Spread the mixture evenly in the prepared tin and spread the remaining walnuts on top. Bake for 20–25 minutes until the cake springs back when lightly pressed. Leave in the tin for 2 minutes, then cut into 16 slices. Transfer to a wire rack to cool.

ORANGE AND HONEY TEABREAD V

Makes one 900-g (2-lb) loaf

100 g (4 oz) sunflower margarine
3 tbsp clear honey
50 g (2 oz) soft brown sugar
50 g (2 oz) chopped walnuts
3 tbsp orange juice
grated rind of 2 oranges
225 g (8 oz) wholemeal self-raising
  flour
2 eggs
extra clear honey for glaze

Heat the oven to 180°C (350° F) mark 4. Line the base of a greased, 900-g (2-lb) loaf tin. Place all the ingredients in a mixing bowl and beat with a wooden spoon for about 3 minutes until well mixed. Place in the loaf tin. Bake in the centre of the oven for 1¼–1½ hours. Turn out and brush with melted honey. Serve sliced and spread with sunflower margarine.

DATE AND WALNUT LOAF   V

Makes one 450-g (1-lb) loaf

*225 g (8 oz) wholemeal self-raising
  flour*
1 tsp baking powder
50 g (2 oz) sunflower margarine
1 tbsp golden syrup
50 g (2 oz) dates, chopped
50 g (2 oz) walnuts, chopped
100 ml (4 fl oz) milk

Heat the oven to 180°C (350° F) mark 4.
Line the base of a greased, deep 450-g (1-lb)
loaf tin. Put the flour and baking powder
together in a bowl. Add all the ingredients
and beat together with a wooden spoon for
about 2–3 minutes until well mixed. Place
the mixture in the tin and smooth the top.
Bake in the centre of the oven for 1–1¼
hours. Turn out of the tin and cool on a wire
rack.

Serve sliced and spread with sunflower
margarine.

MALT BREAD   V

Makes one 900-g (2-lb) loaf

2 tbsp golden syrup
2 tbsp soft brown sugar
2 tbsp malt
200 ml (7 fl oz) milk
*225 g (8 oz) wholemeal self-raising
  flour*
pinch of salt
150 g (5 oz) mixed dried fruit
1 egg, beaten
1 tsp bicarbonate of soda

Heat the oven to 170°C (325° F) mark 3.
Line the base of a greased 900-g (2-lb) loaf
tin. Place the syrup, sugar and malt in a
saucepan. Add 150 ml (¼ pint) of the milk,
then warm and beat until well blended, but
do not allow to overheat.

Put the flour into a mixing bowl and add
the salt and dried fruit. Add the beaten egg
and malt mixture alternately in small
amounts to the flour, stirring constantly.
Dissolve the bicarbonate of soda in the
remaining milk and add to the mixture,
folding in carefully.

Pour into the prepared tin and bake for 1
hour in the centre of the oven. Turn out and
cool on a wire rack. Serve sliced and spread
with sunflower margarine.

BROWN BREAD   VV

Makes 12–16 rolls or 2 loaves or
   2 pizza bases

15 g (½ oz) fresh yeast or 7 g
   (¼ oz) dried yeast
425 ml (¾ pint) warm water (⅔
   cold + ⅓ boiling)
350 g (12 oz) plain wholemeal flour
350 g (12 oz) strong plain white
   flour
2 tsp salt
1 tbsp corn or sunflower oil
1 tbsp sesame or poppy seeds

Mix the yeast with 3 tablespoonfuls of the warm water in a small basin. Mix the flours together, sprinkle a little on top of the yeast mixture and leave in a warm place until it becomes frothy. Mix the remaining flour with the salt and oil. Add the yeast mixture and most of the remaining water. Mix to a soft dough adding all the water if necessary. Knead on a lightly floured surface for about 5–10 minutes until the dough is smooth and elastic.

Place in a lightly greased bowl. Cover and leave to rise until the dough has doubled in size (about 1½ hours) in a warm place, 2½–3 hours at room temperature, or overnight in a greased polythene bag in the refrigerator.

Heat the oven to 230°C (450°F) mark 8. Turn out the dough on to a lightly floured surface and knead for a few minutes. Shape into 12–16 small rolls or 2 fairly wide loaves and place on a greased baking tray. Brush with water, and sprinkle on the sesame seeds or poppy seeds. Cover with a clean cloth and leave in a warm place for 15–20 minutes to prove. Bake for 10 minutes then turn the oven temperature down to 200°C (400°F) mark 6 for a further 5–20 minutes depending on the size.

Variations
(1) All wholemeal flour can be used, in which case it will need 25 g (1 oz) yeast and an extra 2 tablespoonfuls water.
(2) Use ⅓ wholemeal flour, ⅓ granary flour and ⅓ strong white flour with extra yeast and water as above.
(3) When the yeast and water have been added to flour, add 1 large onion, finely grated, together with all the liquid from the

onion and 2 tablespoonfuls chopped fresh
sage, thyme or parsley. This gives a
well-flavoured loaf or rolls which are
delicious served with soup or cheese.

BROWN CROISSANTS   V

Makes 8

15 g (½ oz) fresh yeast or 7 g (¼ oz)
    dried yeast
3 tbsp warm water (⅔ cold and ⅓
    boiling)
1 tsp granulated sugar
100 g (4 oz) plain strong white flour
100 g (4 oz) plain wholemeal flour
½ tbsp salt
1 tbsp corn or sunflower oil
1 egg, beaten
150 g (5 oz) butter
egg and water mixture to glaze

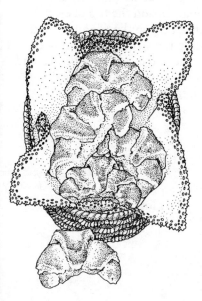

Mix the yeast and warm water together in a
small bowl, add the sugar and sprinkle in
25 g (1 oz) of the white flour. Leave in a
warm place until the mixture is frothy
(about 10–15 minutes).

In a large bowl, mix the wholemeal flour,
the remaining white flour, the oil, the
beaten egg and the salt. When the yeast is
frothy, add to the flour and mix, adding
water if necessary to make a soft dough.

On a floured board, roll out the dough to
a rectangle about 20 x 30 cm (8 x 12
inches). Cut the butter into 1-cm (½-inch)
cubes and place half the cubes, evenly
spaced out, on the top two-thirds of the
dough. Fold the rectangle in thirds and seal.
Roll out and fold in thirds again. Roll out
again and place the remaining butter on the
top two-thirds of the dough; fold and roll
out. Fold and place in a greased polythene
bag. Either leave overnight in the
refrigerator or for 2–3 hours at room
temperature until well risen.

Heat the oven to 200°C (400°F) mark 6.
Roll out the dough into a circle and divide
into 8 triangles. Roll up each triangle from
the outer edge of the circle inwards, towards
the point. Cover with greased polythene and
leave to prove on a greased baking tray for
20–30 minutes, brush with the egg glaze
and bake for 15–20 minutes.

COUNTRY BREAD   V

Makes 2 loaves

450 g (1 lb) plain wholewheat flour
100 g (4 oz) rye flour
100 g (4 oz) cornmeal
2 tsp salt
275 ml (½ pint) milk
2 tbsp black treacle
150 ml (¼ pint) water
15 g (½ oz) fresh yeast or 7 g (¼ oz)
*   dried yeast*

Mix the flours, cornmeal and salt in a large mixing bowl. Place the milk, treacle and water in a small saucepan and cook over a gentle heat until the treacle has melted and the mixture is warm but not hot. Place the yeast in a bowl, gradually add the warm milk mixture and mix until well blended. Pour the yeast liquid on to the dry ingredients and mix until a sticky dough is formed. Turn the dough on to a lightly floured board and knead for about 10 minutes until the dough is no longer sticky, adding more flour if necessary.

Put the dough in a lightly greased bowl. Cover with greased polythene and leave in a warm place for 1–1½ hours until it has doubled in size.

Heat the oven to 200°C (400°F) mark 6. When the dough has risen, turn out and knead for about 5 minutes. Cut the dough in half and shape into 2 oval loaves. Place the loaves on a greased baking tray and make 3 diagonal cuts on the top of each. Cover with greased polythene and leave to rise until doubled in size. Bake for 30–40 minutes until the loaves are dark brown and sound hollow when tapped underneath. Cool on a wire rack.

SCENTED GERANIUM LEAF CAKES   V

Makes 18

18 scented geranium leaves (rose,
  lemon or orange flavour) or 18
  lemon balm leaves
100 g (4 oz) sunflower margarine
100 g (4 oz) soft brown sugar
2 eggs
100 g (4 oz) wholewheat self-raising
  flour
icing sugar to finish

Heat the oven to 190°C (375°F) mark 5. Put paper cases in 18 patty tins. Place the geranium leaf or lemon balm leaf in each paper case. Cream the margarine and sugar and beat in the eggs one at a time, adding 1 teaspoonful flour with the second egg. Beat very thoroughly.

Sieve the flour into the mixture then tip in the bran that is left in the sieve as well, and fold in. Spoon the mixture into the paper cases and bake for 10–15 minutes at the top of the oven. Cool on a wire rack and dredge with icing sugar.

Variation
This mixture can be used for a Victoria sandwich. Use two 15-cm (6-inch) greased, bottom-lined cake tins with scented geranium leaves on the lining paper. Bake in the centre of the oven for 20–25 minutes. Cool and fill with strawberry jam.

COOKIES   VV

Makes 18–20

100 g (4 oz) sunflower margarine
50 g (2 oz) soft brown sugar
150 g (5 oz) wholemeal self-raising
  flour
25 g (1 oz) desiccated coconut or
  chopped nuts or finely grated rind
  of 1 orange or lemon

Heat the oven to 180°C (350°F) mark 4. Cream the margarine and sugar together and fold in the flour. Add the coconut, nuts or orange or lemon rind to the mixture. Form into balls about the size of walnuts and place on a greased baking tray. Press a fork over the top of each ball to flatten slightly. Bake in the centre of the oven for 10–15 minutes, then cool.

These cookies will keep extremely well in an airtight tin. It is worth making double the quantity, dividing the mixture in half and adding a different flavour to each half.

CHERRY AND BANANA LOAF   V

Makes one 900-g (2-lb) loaf

50 g (2 oz) glacé cherries
25 g (1 oz) walnuts
225 g (8 oz) wholemeal self-raising
    flour
100 g (4 oz) sunflower margarine
175 g (6 oz) soft brown sugar
125 g (4 oz) sultanas
4 ripe bananas
2 eggs

Heat the oven to 170°C (325°F) mark 3.
Line the base of a greased, 900-g (2-lb) loaf
tin. Chop the cherries and walnuts and
place all the ingredients in a mixing bowl.
Beat well with a wooden spoon for 2–3
minutes.

Place in the prepared tin and bake in the
centre of the oven for 1¼–1½ hours. Turn
out, remove the paper and cool on a wire
rack. Serve sliced and spread with
sunflower margarine.

HAZELNUT SHORTCAKE   V

Serves 8

Base
75 g (3 oz) sunflower margarine
50 g (2 oz) muscovado sugar
100 g (4 oz) plain wholemeal flour
75 g (3 oz) hazelnuts, roasted and
    ground
egg white to glaze
1 tbsp chopped hazelnuts

Filling
450 g (1 lb) dessert apples, peeled,
    cored and sliced
2 tbsp apple juice
50 g (2 oz) sultanas
50 g (2 oz) raisins
1 tsp mixed spice

Heat the oven to 190°C (375°F) mark 5.
Beat together the margarine and sugar until
soft.

Stir in the flour and ground hazelnuts and
mix to a firm dough. Turn onto a floured
surface and knead lightly until smooth.
Divide in half and roll each piece into a
20-cm (8-inch) diameter round and place on
a baking sheet.

Brush one round with egg white and
sprinkle it with the chopped hazelnuts.
Bake both rounds for 10–15 minutes.

Cut the nut-covered round into 8 sections
while still warm. Transfer both rounds to a
wire rack to cool.

To make the filling, place the apples and
juice in a pan, cover and cook gently for 15
minutes, stirring occasionally. Add the
remaining ingredients and leave to cool.
Spread over the plain round and arrange the
nut-covered sections on top. Serve with
natural yoghurt.

COTTAGE CHEESE TEABREAD V

Makes one 900-g (2-lb) loaf

225 g (8 oz) cottage cheese
175 g (6 oz) soft brown sugar
3 eggs
100 g (4 oz) stoned dates
50 g (2 oz) toasted hazelnuts or
  walnuts
225 g (8 oz) wholemeal self-raising
  flour

Heat the oven to 180°C (350° F) mark 4. Grease a 900-g (2-lb) loaf tin and line with greased greaseproof paper.

Sieve the cottage cheese into a mixing bowl, add the sugar and beat until creamy. Add the eggs one at a time and beat into the mixture. Chop the dates and nuts and fold into the mixture. Add the flour and fold in. Spoon the mixture into the prepared tin and level the surface.

Bake in the centre of the oven for 50–60 minutes until firm and golden brown. Turn out and cool on a wire rack. Serve sliced and spread with sunflower margarine.

Using cottage cheese instead of margarine or butter produces a beautifully light, moist teabread.

WHOLEMEAL FRUIT SCONES   V

Makes about 10

100 g (4 oz) self-raising flour
2 tsp baking powder
100 g (4 oz) plain wholemeal flour
50 g (2 oz) sunflower margarine
25 g (1 oz) glacé cherries, chopped
25 g (1 oz) hazelnuts, chopped
25 g (1 oz) soft brown sugar
8 tbsp milk
milk or egg to glaze

Heat the oven to 220°C (425°F) mark 7. Sieve the self-raising flour and baking powder together and place with the wholemeal flour and margarine in a mixing bowl. Rub in the margarine. Add the sugar, fruit and nuts and mix well. Add the milk and form into a soft dough. Turn on to a lightly floured surface and knead until smooth. Roll out until it is 1 cm (½ inch) thick and cut into rounds with a 5-cm (2-inch) fluted cutter.

Place on a greased baking sheet. Brush with milk or egg glaze. Bake on the top shelf of the oven for 10–15 minutes then cool on a wire rack.

Serve spread with sunflower margarine, or freeze to use later.

Variation
This recipe can be varied by substituting 50 g (2 oz) sultanas or raisins for the cherries and hazelnuts.

OAT FINGERS   VV

Makes 16

4 tbsp corn oil
3 tbsp malt extract
50 g (2 oz) muscovado sugar
225 g (8 oz) rolled oats
2 tbsp sesame seeds, roasted

Heat the oven to 180°C (350°F) mark 4. Place the oil, malt extract and sugar in a saucepan and heat gently. Add the oats and sesame seeds and mix carefully. Press into a greased, 20-cm (8-inch) square shallow tin and level the top with a palette knife. Bake in the centre of the oven for 30 minutes. Cool in the tin for 2 minutes, then cut into fingers. Allow to cool completely before removing from the tin.

HERB AND CHEESE SCONES   V

Makes about 10

100 g (4 oz) self-raising white flour
2 tsp baking powder
100 g (4 oz) plain wholemeal flour
pinch of salt
a good shake of paprika
50 g (2 oz) sunflower margarine
75 g (3 oz) cheese, finely grated
2 tsp chopped fresh chives
2 tsp chopped fresh tarragon
8 tbsp milk
egg or milk to glaze

Heat the oven to 220°C (425° F) mark 7. Sieve the self-raising flour and baking powder together and place with the wholemeal flour in a mixing bowl. Add the salt and paprika and rub in the margarine. Add the cheese, chives and tarragon. Mix to a soft dough with the milk and turn out on to a lightly floured board. Knead lightly.

Roll out to a thickness of 1 cm (½ inch) and cut out rounds using a 5-cm (2-inch) plain cutter. Brush with beaten egg or milk. Place on a greased baking tray and bake for 10–15 minutes at the top of the oven. Cool on a wire rack and serve spread with sunflower margarine.

Variation
Replace the chives and tarragon with 1 tablespoonful chopped fresh oregano or marjoram.

OATMEAL AND HONEY COOKIES   VV

Makes 16

100 g (4 oz) medium oatmeal
100 g (4 oz) plain wholemeal flour
pinch of sea salt
75 g (3 oz) sunflower margarine
2 tbsp clear honey
juice of ½ lemon
16 whole blanched almonds

Heat the oven to 170°C (325° F) mark 3. Place the oatmeal, flour and salt in a mixing bowl. Put the margarine, honey and lemon juice into a saucepan and melt together over a low heat. Make a well in the flour and oatmeal mixture; pour in the honey and margarine mixture and mix thoroughly.

Press the mixture into a greased 18-cm (7-inch) square tin to a thickness of about 1 cm (½ inch). Cut into squares and press a blanched almond on to the centre of each biscuit. Bake for 50 minutes. Leave to cool in the tin for about 15 minutes, then lift on to a wire cooling rack.

DIGESTIVE BISCUITS V

Makes about 22

175 g (6 oz) plain wholemeal flour
50 g (2 oz) fine oatmeal
½ tsp salt
1 tsp baking powder
75 g (3 oz) sunflower margarine
25 g (1 oz) Barbados sugar
3 tbsp milk
1 tbsp sesame seeds

Heat the oven to 190°C (375°F) mark 5. Mix the flour, oatmeal and salt together in a mixing bowl and sieve in the baking powder. Rub in the margarine until the mixture resembles breadcrumbs, then fold in the sugar. Add the milk and mix to form a soft dough.

Turn on to a lightly floured board and roll out thinly. Prick all over with a fork. Cut into 6-cm (2½-inch) rounds with a plain cutter. Brush with water and sprinkle with sesame seeds.

Place on a greased baking tray and cook for 15–20 minutes in the centre of the oven. Transfer to a wire rack to cool.

NUTTY COOKIES VV

Makes 16

75 g (3 oz) soft brown sugar
75 g (3 oz) sunflower margarine
50 g (2 oz) plain flour
50 g (2 oz) hazelnuts, finely
    chopped

Heat the oven to 190°C (375°F) mark 5. Cream the sugar and margarine together until light and fluffy. Stir in the flour and hazelnuts and mix thoroughly. Place small teaspoonfuls of the mixture well apart on greased baking trays and flatten with a damp fork.

Bake for 6–8 minutes until pale golden. Leave on the baking sheets for 1 minute, then remove carefully and leave to cool.

OATCAKES V

Makes 12

175 g (6 oz) fine or medium oatmeal
50 g (2 oz) plain wholemeal flour
2 tsp baking powder

Place the oatmeal and flour in a mixing bowl with the baking powder and salt. Rub in the margarine. Make a well in the centre. Pour in the milk and mix thoroughly to form a dough. Roll out to a thickness of about

1 tsp sea salt
25 g (1 oz) sunflower margarine
150 ml (¼ pint) milk

5 mm (¼ inch) and cut into 5-cm (2-inch) rounds with a plain cutter.

Lightly oil a griddle or heavy frying pan and set on a low to moderate heat. Cook the oatcakes for about 10 minutes on each side or until they are just starting to turn brown and sound slightly hollow when tapped.

OAT & SESAME BISCUITS   V

Makes about 24

75 g (3 oz) rolled oats
50 g (2 oz) medium oatmeal
2 tbsp sesame seeds, roasted or
   grilled
4 tbsp corn or sunflower oil
75 g (3 oz) muscovado sugar
1 egg

Heat the oven to 170°C (325° F) mark 3. Place the oats, oatmeal, sesame seeds, oil and sugar in a bowl and mix thoroughly. Leave to stand for 1 hour. Beat the egg thoroughly and mix in carefuly. Place teaspoonfuls of the mixture well spaced out on a greased baking tray and flatten with a palette knife.

Bake in the cente of the oven for about 20 minutes until golden brown. Leave to cool for 2 minutes, then transfer to a wire rack to cool completely.

WELSH CAKES   V

Makes 16

75 g (3 oz) plain white flour
½ tsp baking powder
pinch of salt
75 g (3 oz) wholemeal flour
¼ tsp mixed spice
50 g (2 oz) currants
75 g (3 oz) sunflower margarine
50 g (2 oz) soft brown sugar
1 egg, beaten

Sieve the white flour, baking powder, spices and salt together. Add the wholemeal flour. Rub in the margarine, add the sugar and currants; mix with the beaten egg. Roll out and cut into 5-cm (2-inch) rounds with a plain cutter. Oil a griddle or cast iron frying pan and cook the cakes until lightly browned on each side.

Serve hot or cold, spread with sunflower margarine.

FRUIT SQUARES   VV

Makes 18

100 g (4 oz) sunflower margarine
175 g (6 oz) plain flour
50 g (2 oz) caster sugar
100 g (4 oz) dates, chopped finely
25 g (1 oz) hazelnuts, toasted and
  chopped or walnuts, chopped
finely grated rind of 1 small orange
1 tbsp clear honey
icing sugar for dredging

Heat the oven to 180°C (350°F) mark 4. Rub the margarine into the flour, add the sugar and knead to form a smooth dough. Press half the mixture into a square 18-cm (7-inch) shallow greased baking tin.

To make the filling, mix the dates, nuts, rind and honey together and spread over the base. Press the remaining dough over the top and bake for about 30 minutes. Cool, cut into squares, then dredge with icing sugar.

YORKSHIRE PARKIN   V

175 g (6 oz) plain wholemeal flour
1½ tsp bicarbonate of soda
1 tsp ground ginger
50 g (2 oz) medium oatmeal
75 g (3 oz) soft brown sugar
100 g (4 oz) golden syrup
75 g (3 oz) sunflower margarine
1 egg, beaten
milk

Heat the oven to 170°C (325°F) mark 3. Put the flour, bicarbonate of soda and ground ginger into a bowl and mix with the oatmeal. Melt the sugar, syrup and margarine in a saucepan and pour over the flour mixture. Add the egg and enough milk to produce a soft consistency. Pour into a tin 18 x 25 cm (7 x 10 inches) lined with greased greaseproof paper and cook for about 1 hour until firm to the touch.

Leave to cool in the tin. When cold, remove and cut into squares. If possible store for 2 weeks in an airtight container before eating.

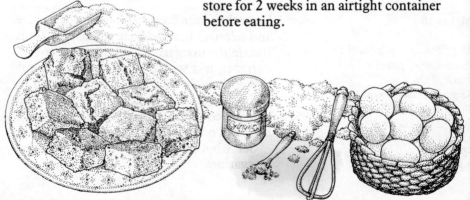

MACAROONS   V

Makes 10

1 large egg white
100 g (4 oz) granulated sugar
50 g (2 oz) ground almonds
1 tsp ground rice
10 split, blanched almonds

Heat the oven to 180°C (350° F) mark 4 and line a baking tray with rice paper or non-stick baking paper.

Whisk the egg white until it forms stiff peaks. Fold in the sugar, ground almonds and ground rice. Place the mixture in a nylon forcing bag fitted with a plain 1-cm (½-inch) nozzle (or use a spoon) and pipe in small rounds on to the paper, spacing the macaroons to allow room for them to expand.

Place a split blanched almond in the centre of each macaroon and bake for 15–20 minutes until they are just beginning to colour. Cool on a wire rack and trim away the excess rice paper.

GINGERBREAD   V

175 g (6 oz) plain white flour
175 g (6 oz) plain wholemeal flour
3 tsp ground ginger
100 g (4 oz) Barbados sugar
250 g (9 oz) golden syrup
175 g (6 oz) sunflower margarine
2 eggs
150 ml (¼ pint) milk
1 tsp bicarbonate of soda

Heat the oven to 180°C (350° F) mark 4. Sieve the plain white flour and ginger into a mixing bowl. Add the wholemeal flour. Melt the sugar, syrup and margarine in a saucepan but do not overheat.

Mix together the eggs, milk and bicarbonate of soda. Make a well in the centre of the flour, add the two liquids alternately, mixing well after each addition. Mix to a soft, pouring consistency and pour into a greased 18 x 25-cm (7 x 10-inch) tin lined with greased greaseproof paper. Bake in the centre of the oven for 50–60 minutes.

Remove from the oven and cool on a wire rack. Store in a tin for a week if possible to allow the gingerbread to mature.

DRESSINGS AND SAUCES

This chapter contains a collection of basic sauce recipes, and explains how to make a variety of salad dressings.

FRENCH DRESSING   VV

2 tbsp cider vinegar or wine vinegar
1 tsp salt
1 tsp freshly ground black pepper
pinch of soft brown sugar
6 tbsp sunflower oil

Place all the ingredients in a screw-topped jar and shake well. Shake again just before pouring over salad.

MINT DRESSING   VV

1 tbsp finely chopped fresh mint
3 tbsp sunflower oil
1 tbsp lemon juice
½ tsp salt
½ tsp freshly ground black pepper
1 tsp soft brown sugar

Put all the ingredients in a screw-topped jar and shake well. Chill for 30 minutes before serving.

Variation
Finely chopped fresh rosemary or lemon balm can be used instead of mint.

YOGHURT DRESSING   V

275 ml (½ pint) natural yoghurt
4 tbsp lemon juice
1 clove garlic, crushed with salt
1 tsp freshly ground black pepper

Place all the ingredients in a small mixing bowl and beat together until thoroughly blended. Use immediately.

SOURED CREAM DRESSING   V

150 ml (¼ pint) soured cream
1 tbsp lemon juice
1 clove garlic, crushed
1 tsp clear honey
salt and freshly ground black pepper
2 tbsp milk (optional)

Place all the ingredients in a bowl and mix thoroughly with a fork. Add a little milk if the dressing is too thick.

MAYONNAISE   V

1 egg or 2 egg yolks
½ tsp salt
½ tsp dry mustard
white pepper
pinch of brown sugar
275 ml (½ pint) sunflower oil
2 tbsp white wine vinegar
2–3 drops each of rosemary and
*   tarragon vinegar (optional)*

Make sure all the ingredients are at room temperature. Place the egg, salt, mustard, pepper and sugar in a bowl and beat well. Add the oil a few drops at a time, beating constantly. Take care not to add the oil too quickly or the mayonnaise will curdle. Once the mixture thickens, the oil may be added in a thin stream.

Mix the white wine vinegar with the herb vinegars if used. Fold in 1 tablespoonful of the vinegar and continue adding the oil, beating well all the time. When all the oil has been added, stir in the remaining vinegar and check the seasoning, adjusting as necessary.

SOY SAUCE DRESSING   VV

150 ml (¼ pint) sunflower or corn oil
3 tbsp soy sauce
2 tbsp lemon juice
1 clove garlic, crushed with salt
freshly ground black pepper

Put all the ingredients in a screw-topped jar and shake well to blend.

CHEESE SAUCE   V

Makes 275 ml (½ pint)

25 g (1 oz) sunflower margarine
25 g (1 oz) plain wholemeal flour
275 ml (½ pint) milk
50 g (2 oz) strong Cheddar cheese,
*   finely grated*
seasoning

Put the margarine, flour and milk into a saucepan and whisk gently over a moderate heat until the sauce thickens. Lower the heat. Add the cheese and mix well. Season to taste.

BÉCHAMEL SAUCE   V

Makes 275 ml (½ pint)

2–3 slices carrot
1 small onion, sliced
1 bay leaf
6 peppercorns
1 piece blade of mace
275 ml (½ pint) milk
25 g (1 oz) sunflower margarine
25 g (1 oz) plain white flour
2 tbsp top of milk

Place the carrot, onion, bay leaf, peppercorns and mace in a saucepan. Add the milk and bring slowly to the boil. Remove the pan from the heat; cover and leave to infuse for 30 minutes. Strain and reserve the liquid. Put the margarine, flour and milk mixture in a saucepan and whisk gently over a moderate heat, until the sauce thickens. Add the top of the milk.

Variations
(1) Mornay sauce. Add 50–75 g (2–3 oz) finely grated cheese to the sauce with the top of the milk.
(2) Soubise sauce. Finely dice and cook 2 onions in 1 tablespoonful corn oil for 10–15 minutes until soft. Add to the basic béchamel sauce.

TOMATO SAUCE   VV

Makes 275–425 ml (½–¾ pint)

1 clove garlic, crushed
450 g (1 lb) tomatoes
2 tbsp sunflower or corn oil
1 tbsp chopped fresh parsley
salt and pepper

Skin and chop the tomatoes. Heat the oil in a saucepan. Add the garlic, tomatoes, parsley and seasoning and simmer for 10 minutes. Liquidise or sieve.

WHAT IS THE WI?

If you have enjoyed this book, the chances are that you would enjoy belonging to the largest women's organisation in the country — the Women's Institute.

We are friendly, go-ahead, like-minded women, who derive enormous satisfaction from all the movement has to offer. This list is long — you can make new friends, have fun and companionship, visit new places, develop new skills, take part in community services, fight local campaigns, become a WI market producer, and play an active role in an organisation which has a national voice.

The WI is the only women's organisation in the country which owns an adult education establishment. At Denman College, you can take a course in anything from car maintenance to paper sculpture, from book-binding to yoga, or cordon bleu cookery to fly-fishing.

All you need to do to join is write to us here at the **National Federation of Women's Institutes, 39 Eccleston Street, London SW1W 9NT**, or telephone 01-730 7212, and we will put you in touch with WIs in your immediate locality. We hope to hear from you.

ABOUT THE AUTHOR

Margaret Hanford, a trained Home Economics teacher, has lectured in training and technical colleges and taught in schools. For several years she has tutored a variety of courses including wholefood cookery at the WI's Denman College.

A WI national cookery and preservation judge, demonstrator and assessor, she belongs to Quorn WI and is adviser to the Home Economics Sub-committee of the Leicestershire and Rutland Federation of Women's Institutes.

INDEX

Aduki Bean Casserole, 41
All-in-one Pastry, 52
 Sweet Flan Pastry, 72
Apple
 Celery and Walnut Salad, 60
 and Blackcurrant Snow, 70
 Flan, 72
 Quorn Apples, 67
Apricot and Mint Pancakes, 50
Autumn Carrots, 55
Avocado Dip, 22

Baked Haddock Steaks, 38
Bean Soup, 18
Béchamel Sauce, 93
Beef
 and Bean Casserole, 30
 and Macaroni, 33
Biscuits
 Digestive, 86
 Oat and Sesame, 87
Blackcurrant
 Clafouti, 71
 Whip, 67
Brazil Nut Patties, 39
Bread
 Brown, 78
 Country, 80
 Malt, 77
Brown Croissants, 79
Brown Rice Salad, 63
Brussels Sprouts
 Soup, 18
 with Almonds, 57

Cabbage
 Salad, 62
 and Grape Salad, 61
 Chinese Cabbage Salad, 62
carbohydrates, 8
Carrot
 and Watercress Salad, 61
 Soup, 17
Cashew Roast, 39
Cauliflower
 Spiced, 56
 Lemon and Herb, 57
Cheese
 Sauce, 92
 Soufflé, 45
Cheese, Tomato and Walnut
 Loaf, 40
Cheesecake

Traditional Cooked, 66
Cherry and Banana Loaf, 82
Chick Pea Curry, 49
Chicken
 and Wholewheat Noodles, 27
 Herb Baked, 28
 Liver Pâté, 23
 Pilaff, 29
 Véronique, 28
Chilled Tomato Soup, 19
Cocktail
 Grape, 21
 Melon, 21
 Prawn and Apple, 19
Concombre Crécy, 57
Cookies, 81
 Nutty, 86
 Oatmeal and Honey, 85
cooking methods, 10
Cottage Cheese Teabread, 83
Country Bread, 80
Courgettes
 with Tomatoes, 56
 Provençale, 58
Croissants
 Brown, 79
Cucumber
 and Yoghurt Soup, 19
 Concombre Crécy, 57
 Cucumber Salad, 62
Curried Eggs, 42

Damson Charlotte, 70
Danish Fruit Trifle, 65
Date and Walnut Loaf, 77
Digestive Biscuits, 86
Dressings
 French, 91
 Mint, 91
 Soured Cream, 91
 Soy Sauce, 92
 Yoghurt, 91
Duchesse Potatoes, 59

Eggs
 Curried, 42
 Florentine, 43
 from Provence, 46
 Potato Baked, 46

fats, 7
fibre, 6
Fish
 Baked Haddock Steaks, 38

Haddock au Gratin, 36
 Kebabs, 37
 Red Beans and Tuna au
  Gratin, 48
 Smoked Haddock Pancakes, 51
 Steaks with Fennel, 36
Flour
 Granary, 7
 Strong Plain White Bread, 7
 Wheatgerm, 7
 Wheatmeal, 7
 Wholemeal, 7
food groups, 5
French Dressing, 91
Fruit
 Crumble, 71
 Salad, 65, 66
 Squares, 88

Gingerbread, 89
Grape
 Cocktail, 21
 Cabbage and Grape Salad, 61
 Snow, 68

Haddock au Gratin, 36
Hazelnut Shortcake, 82
Hearts in Cider, 34
Herb and Cheese Scones, 85
Herb Baked Chicken, 28
Hot Coffee Pudding, 69
Hummus, 16

Khoshaf, 65
Kipper Pâté, 22

lacto-vegetarian, 4
Lamb
 Navarin of, 25
 Loin of Lamb Chops Tartare, 26
 Cutlets and Pepper Sauce, 32
Leek and Rice au Gratin, 48
Lemon
 and Herb Cauliflower, 57
 Delight, 68
Lentil and Spinach Roulade, 47
Lentil Roast, 38
Loaf
 Cheese, Tomato and Walnut, 40
 Date and Walnut, 77
 Mushroom and Nut, 40
Loin of Lamb Chops Tartare, 26

Macaroons, 89
Macaroni
  Beef with, 33
  Carbonara, 44
Malt Bread, 77
Mandarin Custard, 69
Mayonnaise, 92
Melon Cocktail, 21
Melon and Tomato Vinaigrette, 21
minerals, 9, 10
Mint Dressing, 91
measurements, 11
  American equivalents, 11
Mushroom and Nut Loaf, 40
Mushroom Soup, 17

Navarin of Lamb, 25
Nut Pâté, 15
Nutty Cookies, 86

Oat
  and Seasame Biscuits, 87
  Fingers, 84
Oatcakes, 86
Oatmeal and Honey Cookies, 85
Onion Flan, 53
Orange and Honey Teabread, 76

Pancakes
  Apricot and Mint, 50
  Savoury Nut, 51
  Smoked Haddock, 51
  Wholemeal Batter, 50
Pasta
  Accaruna i casa alla Filippino, 33
  Chicken and Wholewheat Noodles, 27
  Macaroni Carbonara, 44
Pastry
  All-in-one, 52
  Sweet Flan, 72
Pâté
  Chicken Liver, 23
  Kipper, 22
  Nut, 15
Peanut Appetisers, 13
Pears
  and Walnut Salad, 20
  Stuffed, 68
  with Cottage Cheese, 20
Pilau, 37
Piperade, 44

Pizza, 53
Pork
  Chops baked in Yoghurt, 26
  Goulash, 35
  with Prunes, 27
Potato Baked Eggs, 46
Potatoes
  Badoise, 60
  Duchesse, 59
  Croquettes, 59
Prawn and Apple, 19
proteins, 8
Pulses, 13
  Aduki Bean Casserole, 41
  Bean Soup, 18
  Beef and Bean Casserole, 30
  Chick Pea Curry, 49
  Lentil Roast, 38
  Lentil and Spinach Roulade, 47
  Red Bean Soup, 16
  Red Beans and Tuna au Gratin, 48
  Sausage and Bean Casseole, 42
  Sweet and Sour Beans, 55

Quorn Apples, 67

Raspberry Flan, 73
Ratatouille, 58
Red Apple and Nut Salad, 63
Red Beans and Tuna au Gratin, 48
Red Bean Soup, 16
Roast
  Cashew, 39
  Lentil, 38

Salad
  Apple, Celery and Walnut, 60
  Brown Rice, 63
  Cabbage, 62
  Cabbage and Grape, 61
  Carrot and Watercress, 61
  Chinese Cabbage, 62
  Cucumber, 62
  Fruit, 65, 66
  Mushroom, 60
  Pear and Walnut, 20
  Red Apple and Nut, 63
Sauces
  Béchamel, 93
  Cheese, 92

Tomato, 93
Sausage and Bean Casserole, 42
Sauté of Kidneys Turbigo, 34
Savoury Cocked Hats, 14
Savoury Liver, 31
Savoury Nut Pancakes, 51
Savoury Quiche, 52
Savoury Walnut Sablés, 14
Scented Gernanium Leaf Cakes, 81
Scones
  Herb and Cheese, 85
  Wholemeal Fruit, 84
Smoked Haddock Pancakes, 51
Soup
  Bean, 18
  Brussels Sprout, 18
  Carrot, 17
  Chilled Tomato, 19
  Cucumber and Yoghurt, 19
  Mushroom, 17
  Red Bean, 16
Soy Sauce Dressing, 92
Soured Cream Dressing, 91
Spiced Cauliflower, 56
Stuffed Pears, 68
Sweet and Sour Beans, 55

Teabread
  Cottage Cheese, 83
  Orange and Honey, 76
Tomato
  Sauce, 93
  Soup, chilled, 19
Trout Mousse, 23
Traditional Cooked Cheesecake, 66
Turkey in Hazelnut Sauce, 30

vegan, 4
vitamins, 9

Walnut and Banana Crunch, 76
Welsh Cakes, 87
Wholemeal
  Flour, 7
Fruit Scones, 84
  Pancake Batter, 50

Yoghurt Dressing, 91
Yorkshire Parkin, 88